ADVANCE PRAISE

"This deeply felt and precisely written story of two young lovers—Bill, undercover for the CIA, and Liz, privileged and openly revolutionary—immerses us in the turmoil of the 1967-70 student protests that lead inexorably to reckless violence and ruthless police repression, testing the breaking point of American democracy. The novel puts us there to show how devotion to altruistic government can go wrong, foster intransigent revolutionary idealism, painfully wither the human heart, and destroy love even as it proclaims saving humanity. This is a vivid story for today, too. The tragedy of Liz and Bill reminds us of our duty to seek fair justice in a world newly yanked apart by zealous, vengeful divisiveness."

— **William Conger**, artist; professor emeritus
art theory & practice
Northwestern University

"Rebellion, Love, Betrayal is a compelling story. Heinz, a renowned scholar in law and the social sciences, has brought his formidable skills to a work of fiction—to the good fortune of his readers. He has produced an important novel concerning the troubling events of 1968 as well as an enjoyable read."

— **Irvin Slate**, retired lawyer
Hot Springs, AK

"The novel artfully draws the reader into a respectful engagement with the antagonistic characters. It makes us like them before we undertake to judge them. We find no clichéd vilification of the CIA honcho in Langley, even as he orchestrates the undercover operation central to the plot; no dark caricatures of antiwar activists as bloodthirsty anarchists, even as they plot boneheaded acts of violent resistance; and no sanctimony from the protagonist, even as he struggles with irreconcilable loyalties to his CIA employer on the one hand and his activist-lover on the other. Each character is credibly human, so we hear them out.

D1502104

And we find they have a lot to say about a complicated and still-painful chapter in American history."

—David A. Collins, JD, PhD
former president of the American Bar Foundation

"Jack Heinz masterfully combines the eye of an historian with the insight of a novelist dealing with the complexity of characters. Through Bill and Liz and their relationship, the novel explores the political, social, and moral issues that the tumultuous period of 1967-1970 raised. Those who lived through that period, and those who want to understand the issues raised then that have helped to shape our current attitudes, should find this novel fascinating."

—Rayman Solomon, JD, PhD
former Provost
Rutgers University, Camden

"In *Rebellion, Love, Betrayal,* Jack Heinz takes us into the hearts and minds of young Americans who were simply trying to do what was right during a time when it was hard to know what was right. Through the eyes of Heinz's characters, we learn about the politics of the Vietnam War era, on all sides, in compelling terms. This is a "must read" for anyone interested in the history of that era. You can't leave this book without looking more deeply into your own convictions about freedom, loyalty, and, most of all, love."

—Linda Hughes, award-winning author of
Secrets of the Summer

REBELLION,
LOVE,
BETRAYAL

REBELLION, LOVE, BETRAYAL

a novel

Jack Heinz

for Washington University, with thanks for many lessons (all of them needed).

Jack Heinz

Deeds Publishing | Athens

May 2019

Published by Deeds Publishing in Athens, GA
www.deedspublishing.com

Printed in The United States of America

Cover design by Mark Babcock. Text layout by Matt King.
Cover photograph and interior photographs courtesy of Bill Hood. Copyright ©2019 Bill Hood.

Library of Congress Cataloging-in-Publications data is available uponrequest.

ISBN 978-1-947309-77-7

Books are available in quantity for promotional or premium use. For information, email info@deedspublishing.com.

First Edition, 2019

10 9 8 7 6 5 4 3 2 1

"*Men must be capable of imagining and executing and insisting on social change, if they are to reform or even maintain civilization, and capable too of furnishing the rebellion which is sometimes necessary if society is not to perish of immobility. Therefore all men should have a drop of treason in their veins, if the nations are not to go soft like so many sleepy pears.*"

— Rebecca West, *The New Meaning of Treason* (1964)

One

There was pressure from the crowd behind her. Protesters were trying to get closer to the building, and soldiers were struggling to hold them back. Most of the marchers were young. They pushed. The soldiers and local police pushed back, but they were not using their weapons, not yet. Federal marshals employed by the U. S. Department of Justice, however, were more aggressive. They were armed with clubs that they called "batons," and they used them.

Then the crowd broke through a fence five yards away from her. Students started streaming through and the marshals were swinging their clubs. She moved to get out of the way, but a boy next to her was hit on the head and knocked unconscious. She tried to help him; he didn't respond. Two students serving as medics picked up the boy and carried him away. She started to follow them, but a marshal threatened to hit her. She didn't know why. Then a dozen, perhaps twenty, of the protesters broke through the police and military lines and ran up the steps of the Pentagon to the main entrance. Some of them got in. The invad-

1

ers were soon caught, brought out in handcuffs, and taken to vans waiting for prisoners, but the invasion had succeeded.

The march started more quietly. Liz thought that the first part, across Memorial Bridge, was pleasant because of the breeze off the Potomac, but the long slog along the parkway was a drag. The Pentagon had seemed closer to the Memorial on a trip to Washington to see the cherry blossoms. Of course that was riding in a car. She saw now that she should have worn sneakers. It can be hot in Washington in late October. Fortunately, the day was only in the high sixties. Estimates of the number of marchers varied. Some said that there were 50,000; some said 100,000. Either way, it was crowded. This made for camaraderie, and also for body odor. Some of these hippies didn't bathe.

The march was led by Abbie Hoffman and Jerry Rubin. Their Youth International Party ("the Yippies") wasn't put together yet, but the essential element, the spirit, was there. Liz liked Abbie—from afar; she had never met him. He was charismatic and sort of cuddly, friendly. Jerry was dour. Maybe Jerry just had a lot on his mind. There was certainly much to be upset about. The news reported that thousands were being killed, both Americans and Vietnamese.

When Liz's group got to the Pentagon, they were told to assemble in North Parking. It was a big area, but it wasn't big enough to hold all the marchers. They looked for places to stand, or sit—there was seldom enough room to lie down. A lot of them were smoking dope. The police, and there were plenty of them, were more concerned with keeping the demonstrators corralled. Dope was a different issue, not at the top of their list. Surrounding the building, all the way around as far as Liz could see, was a line of uniformed officers. Behind the police, soldiers with rifles were reinforced by barriers, sawhorses, and temporary fences. There were men with binoculars and cameras on the roof of the Pentagon.

Hippie girls had brought flowers. Liz didn't approve of it; this wasn't a celebration. If there was irony in bringing flowers to the Pentagon, Liz didn't get it. Some girls walked right up to the line of soldiers and put flowers into the barrels of their rifles. The soldiers were annoyed. Newspaper photographers loved it. It would be on the front page the next day. If the gesture was meant to be disrespectful, that was fine, Liz supposed, but it seemed silly.

Some of the students behaved as if it were a big party. Liz didn't see it that way. Facing armed police and soldiers was serious, maybe dangerous, and the purpose of the march was certainly serious. Liz thought that the war was wrong, morally wrong. It needed to end. She would bear a lot more pain than the blisters on her feet if that would help to end the war.

The breeze off the Potomac grew colder. Army Reserve troops who had been on the line for several hours were replaced by seasoned soldiers who had served in Vietnam. The new men were not in a mood to tolerate disrespect. And Liz was chilly. The afternoon had been warm, but now she wanted a heavier jacket—the windbreaker was too thin. She wasn't sure whether she was stamping her feet to stay warm or because of the tension of the confrontation.

Four of her friends from the Ann Arbor chapter of Students for a Democratic Society, including Hal and BJ, were nearby. SDS had been founded at the University of Michigan and it was strong there. Earlier in the day, Hal had joined a group of men burning their draft cards down at the Justice Department. Liz gave him a kiss as a reward. She enjoyed the kiss. He enjoyed it more. BJ was too old for the draft, but he was active in the principal organization behind the march, the National Mobilization Committee to End the War in Vietnam ("the Mobe"). Liz thought that BJ's ties to the leaders might be helpful if she was arrested.

By nightfall, police started making arrests enthusiastically, mostly for failure to move when ordered to do so or for disturbing the peace. When the protest ended, 683 demonstrators had been arrested and hundreds had been taken to hospitals. Liz was not charged and was unharmed.

Late 1967, Langley, Virginia

A small sign at the exit from the George Washington Parkway said, "Bureau of Public Roads," and there may have been a BPR office somewhere in the general vicinity, but most people who lived in the area knew that the big building was the headquarters of the Central Intelligence Agency. The CIA had recruited Bill Burke on a college campus—standard practice—in his case in his senior year at Rochester. He was then trained for covert assignments. The Agency's curriculum covered "tradecraft" such as dead letter boxes, eavesdropping, evasive maneuvers, the recruitment and maintenance of assets, and the techniques of unarmed combat, including lethal options.

He had expected an assignment abroad. But in November, after the completion of his training, he was ordered to report to the

Director of Domestic Operations, Charles Maranville. Bill was both puzzled and disappointed. The domestic section was looking for a young, promising, rather scholarly agent, someone who might fit in on a campus. The violence at the Pentagon and the number of demonstrators had alarmed President Johnson and Robert McNamara, the Secretary of Defense. In response, they had created an interagency working group to monitor and crack down on student radicals. The FBI, the Defense Department, the National Security Agency, and the CIA were all represented in the group.

As Bill approached Mr. Maranville's office at Langley, he heard two men talking in the hall. One said, "Rabbit Maranville is insisting on it." This was a surprise. "Rabbit"! It was the CIA, for God's sake. So much for the dignity of the Director of Domestic Operations. Rabbits are little creatures that are easily frightened. Why would Maranville's colleagues call him that? Bill didn't know what to expect.

In the interview, the Director's first question concerned Bill's employment history. "I see that you worked for a time in a band called 'The New Wolverines.' What did you play?"

"I played saxophone."

"I assume you know that the Wolverines was the name of Bix Beiderbecke's band."

"Yes, sir, I do."

"What was your book?"

"We played the twenties and thirties classics — Louis Armstrong's Hot Fives and Hot Sevens, the New Orleans Rhythm Kings, McKinney's Cotton Pickers."

"The classics." The Director paused and raised his line of sight to a foot or two above Bill's head. "When I was at Princeton, I was in the Triangle Club band and we played the same material. I play piano."

Burke and Maranville talked jazz instead of tradecraft and the interview went smoothly. "Tiger Rag" was no longer a radical statement, but music was, after all, at the center of the youth culture. Most of the new music wasn't jazz, not even close, but it had some of the rebellious spirit of, say, Cab Calloway. Rabbit thought that Burke was young enough and hip enough to fit in with the rock generation.

As Burke was leaving the Director's office, he said, "I know that in the Ellington band Johnny Hodges is sometimes called 'Rabbit.' Did he get that name first, or were you the original?" Maranville's laugh was subdued. "I got the name when I was a boy. There was a famous baseball player called Rabbit Maranville. He was a shortstop—played for the Boston Braves and the St. Louis Cardinals. So, if you were a Maranville, the kids in your school were going to call you Rabbit. It stuck." In truth, the Director disliked the nickname. Inevitably, it had generated comments by fraternity wits to the general effect that he climaxed quickly, too quickly. Apart from some annoyance and embarrassment when he was young, however, the teasing did little harm.

The Director was a serious man, and he looked and acted the part. He played piano with enthusiasm, but with restraint and taste. He had also played football with restraint and taste. The Lake Forest Academy did not have a team of bruisers. Rabbit was not a large man. In his maturity, he had light brown hair going gray, thinning on top. He wore sober glasses, a gentleman's spectacles, tortoise shell, and he dressed like a lawyer from the corporate hemisphere of the profession—which, indeed, was what he had been before the war. General "Wild Bill" Donovan, the director of the OSS (Office of Strategic Services), spotted Lt. Commander Maranville in naval intelligence, and Rabbit went to the CIA soon after it was created.

Bill Burke found Maranville to be a pleasant man, polite, personable, quiet in manner, but rather bland. It was surprising that he was a jazz musician. It was also surprising that he was a spook. Perhaps that made him the perfect spy. There was no hint of the James Bond insouciance or derring-do. No one would suspect him. But Burke didn't really know what Rabbit *did*. Maybe he was just a paper shuffler. Maybe he just prepared budgets and attended the parties of the diplomatic corps. There were, of course, things to be learned in D.C. simply by moving about and keeping your ears open. Many of those things were untrue, but it was a part of the job to sort that out.

It was clear that Maranville held his cards close to his vest. After having worked with him for six months, however, Burke made an attempt to draw him out. They had gone to Blues Alley to hear Jay McShann, a wonderful Kansas City pianist. During a break, and after some scotch, Burke said, "So, Rabbit, during the McCarthy era did you spend your time chasing Reds?" It was probably not the best approach.

Rabbit replied. "Have I ever told you that I sometimes have jam sessions at my apartment with old-time players?"

"No, you haven't." Bill stirred his scotch on the rocks with a finger.

Rabbit sipped from his drink. "A few of the true greats of early jazz are still around—Armstrong, Benny Goodman, Bud

Freeman. I don't know Armstrong, but I know Benny and Bud. They sometimes come by. Bud is a jazz sax pioneer out of Chicago. You probably know his work."

Bill said, "I know that he was the leader of a combo called the Summa Cum Laude, which Eddie Condon insisted on calling the Some Came Loaded."

Rabbit nodded. "I know Bud, and I like him. Odd duck. Fancies himself an English gentleman. Dresses like one. Adopts the manner. But he grew up on the north side of Chicago. It's said that Lester Young carried one of Freeman's early records around with him. Listened to it over and over. Quite a tribute." Rabbit ordered another scotch and soda and loosened his shirt collar. "I never knew what to make of Lester Young. Another odd duck. He was certainly strange."

Burke agreed. "Lester, 'the President', Prez. My friend Alfred Appel went to see Prez at a New York club. After the club closed for the night, Alfred saw Prez standing at a street corner, either waiting for a taxi or waiting to cross. Alfred had a car, and he didn't drink, so he offered Prez a ride home. Prez looked at him carefully and said, 'Thank you, Lady Kindness, but the President has wheels'. Prez called Billie Holliday 'Lady Day,' and he was inclined to bestow the compliment more widely. His grasp of gender was always tenuous."

McShann returned to the piano, went into "Moten Swing," and the McCarthy era wasn't mentioned again.

Early 1968, Ann Arbor, Michigan

Langley's expert on the Midwest, Tom Rasmussen, said that Fourth and Pitner was the place to go. Bill had been told to look for a bar near that corner. The neighborhood was down at the heels. Modest houses, built for families in the last century, were cut-up into apartments for students. The brick sidewalks were uneven after many decades of freezing and thawing, and gaps in the brickwork were filled with asphalt. A few small businesses had space in some of the houses, usually with a business below and apartments above.

Bill walked into a basement music dive. The sign out front said that Dave Van Ronk was coming the previous week. The sign was still there — Van Ronk was a big event for this joint. It was three steps below street level in the "English basement" of an old house. The exposed brick walls were painted black, outside and in, and it was dark in the club. The black walls absorbed the light. There was no mistaking the smell of grass in the smoke fog. Bill could see open space at the bar. He ordered a beer.

The bartender was a young woman. Not bad, he thought. In fact, better than that. Probably a student at the U. He didn't take her in all at once, but he noted her figure (nice), her eyes (large and hazel), and her hair (light brown), long enough for a wayward lock to fall across her forehead. She wasn't fussy about it. She looked healthy — more healthy than you would expect for a girl who tends bar. She was friendly. Bill wiped off the neck of the bottle with his hand.

She asked, "You want a glass?"

"No thanks. Don't need it."

9

The beer was Leinenkugel's Chippewa Pride. He read the label: "Made with water from the Big Eddy Spring." Bill had never heard of it. It was okay.

Bill said, "It's dark in here."

She nodded, "Yep, darker than the inside of a cow."

"That's colorful."

She looked at the bar rag in her hand. "This is the Midwest. We have to try harder to find colorful regionalisms." She took another look at him. "Haven't seen you around. You here for Voice?"

"Just got to Ann Arbor yesterday. What's Voice?"

Bill, in fact, knew what Voice was, but he wanted to see what response he would get. Langley had briefed him: Voice had been, originally, a student political party at the University, and it had evolved into the local branch of SDS. The bar was a gathering place for its members.

The bartender's reply was cautious, guarded. Who was this guy? "Oh, politics. Just a bunch of people who talk politics."

Bill pursued it. "I'm interested in politics. How do I find those people?"

"This place is full of them. Just make some friends. Have another beer or two."

"Do you have anything besides Leinenkugel's?"

"Nope."

"Okay." Bill introduced himself. "I'm Willy, Willy Feld."

"Feld sounds Jewish. I wouldn't have taken you for Jewish."

"Yeah, well there was a lot of sleeping around." Bill took a swig of beer, but she didn't reply. "Are you a student of such things?"

"Of what, of sleeping around?"

"No, of ancestry, ethnicity, figuring out who people are."

"I'm an anthropologist. I'm an expert on inherited culture, but right now I have to serve some more beer."

Bill waited while she opened four bottles for a customer at the other end of the bar. He thought she might stay down there, but she returned. Bill took a closer look so that he would be able to describe her in his report. Mid-twenties, white, medium build, maybe about 5'7", three or four inches shorter than he was. She was dressed ten percent bartender and ninety percent grad student. White shirt, a necklace of Indian beads, jeans, sandals. No makeup. Her nose was thin and elegant, her features sharp and symmetrical.

He smiled. "You haven't told me your name."

"I'm Liz."

"You worked here long?"

"About seven months now."

"Do you like the job, tending bar?"

"It pays the rent."

"Doesn't dealing with drunks get to be a hassle?"

"We don't get many drunks in here."

"How about guys hitting on you?"

"I can handle that... You ask a lot of questions."

"I was leading up to this one: Do anthropologists ever go out on dates?"

"You know where to find me."

Then another customer wanted a beer.

Walking back to the small apartment that Langley had arranged, Bill wondered about Liz. Would she be a useful source? She didn't say much about Voice or SDS. How close is she to the leaders? Is she an insider? Who's she living with? A romantic involvement with her already seems like a possibility, maybe—if she's willing. But Rabbit discourages emotional attachments that distort judgment.

Bill walked some more and he thought some more. She has beautiful hair. There's a certain light in her eyes. She's smart, I think—clever. I liked the cow. But I need to remember that this is a job, not summer vacation. She might provide a route to acceptance in the group. The people in that bar have to like me. The Agency wants me to cultivate sources. There's no way I can do the job without sources. She might well be useful, so there's no reason I shouldn't try to cultivate her…In the line of duty? That sounds pretty cold, calculating.

But who am I kidding? I like her—I'm attracted to her. And I don't want to hurt her. Still, I have a job to do. Am I using the job as an excuse? An excuse for what? For courting her? I don't need any excuse for that, except to shield me from Rabbit. Liz and I are both free, mostly. She's a mature adult…What the hell! I like her. I think I should do what comes naturally. If the relationship gets too close it'll be uncomfortable, but the Agency never promised me that this would all be comfortable.

April 1968, Ann Arbor, the bar

Bill asked her, "You like Chinese?"

"Yes."

"How about the Cathay Gardens?"

"Never been there. Terrible name."

"Standard name. Standard food. One from column A, one from column B, with two you get eggroll."

Liz laughed. "Sounds wonderful." They went outside, and Liz spoke again. "Why is it that Jewish guys always like Chinese food? Is it because potstickers are like knishes?"

Bill stopped long enough for Liz to take two steps. "So, do you have any name besides Liz?"

"Watson."

"What would a Liz Watson know about knishes? Did Ellis Island or the family business change your name?" They left the campus, turned toward the business district, and walked in silence for a minute or two. Then Bill said, "I have a confession to make."

Without breaking stride, Liz replied, "No doubt more than one."

"No, only one, for now. Actually it's not a confession. It's just that you made an assumption. I'm not Jewish. I'm mostly Irish."

"Where did the name Feld come from?"

"One of my ancestors was afraid he'd be discriminated against because of being Irish, so he changed his name, but he made a bad choice."

Liz laughed again. "He wasn't an anthropologist."

"No, he sure wasn't. Or a historian, or a sociologist, or much of anything else."

The restaurant wasn't crowded. They ordered one princess chicken (hot) and one large noodle soup with two bowls. They would share.

Bill smiled. "So, where were you before Ann Arbor?"

"At college, at Bryn Mawr."

"And before that?"

"At the Upperville School, in Virginia."

Bill picked up the menu again. "Is the soup and the chicken going to be enough?"

"It will for me."

"Okay. What's the Upperville School?"

"A girls' prep school."

"Oh. Where?"

"It's in the Virginia hunt country. There was a lot of interest in horses."

"Swell. So you're an East Coaster?"

"No, I was born and raised in a small town in northern Illinois."

"Bryn Mawr and the Upperville School are both fancy. Apart from being smart, how does a small-town girl from the Midwest find her way to those places?"

"You're pretty good at cross-examining." Liz understood what he was asking. "The truth is that my family owns the local bank in that small town."

Bill raised his eyebrows. "But you and your buddies in Voice, including me, want to dispossess the ruling class. Have you always wanted to stick it to them?"

"No." Liz looked uncomfortable and lowered her voice. "When I first arrived at Bryn Mawr, I was a Republican. I spoke up for Nixon and wanted to get rid of Social Security and the estate tax when all of my friends were backing Jack Kennedy."

"What happened?"

"You know what happened. The assassination of Dr. King, the Bay of Pigs, the bombing of women and children in Vietnam, the violence of the cops at Columbia, a Ku Klux Klan cell in the Chicago Police Department. The corruption and violence and immorality of the ruling regime became so obvious that no honest person could ignore it."

"Well said. You're a fine person, Liz. Whatever your family taught you, you've directed it down the right path."

"Wow! That's a romantic seduction line if I ever heard one. You sure know how to flatter a girl." Liz poured more tea into her little cup.

"I'm serous, Liz."

"No doubt about that. Whatever else you may be, Willy Feld or whatever in hell your name is, there's sure no doubt that you're serious."

Bill was taken aback. He wondered whether Liz knew more than she was saying. But how could she? The Agency had provided a good cover. He needed to keep his cool and not blow it.

"My background is different from yours. I'm from the other side of the tracks, in Brooklyn, shanty Irish. I went to Colgate on a scholarship, and I was lucky to get that. I don't have as much to lose as you do, or did, but I share your assessment of the state of our government. We need to change it. And it's pretty clear that our generation has to do it."

"Were you at the Pentagon?"

Bill flinched and said, "What?"

"The march on the Pentagon last fall—were you there?"

It was a bad moment. Bill should have realized that she meant the October Peace March, which had turned into a confrontation with armed troops. He struggled to recover.

"No. Were you?"

"Yes." She looked at him sternly.

Bill decided to take the offensive. "Did you get arrested?" It was a question of your creds, just as her's had been.

"No, but I barely avoided getting hit by a marshal's club."

"I heard that seven hundred people, mostly students, were arrested."

"Yeah, and more than that were beaten. The soldiers mostly didn't do anything except form a line—I think they didn't want to hit kids who looked like them—but the federal marshals were godawful. Fascists."

"The newspapers said that the charge by the SDS and the Yippies took the soldiers by surprise."

She smiled. "Yeah. The Pentagon looked weak. It scared the crap out of McNamara and Johnson."

Bill knew that was true. It was how he came to be in Ann Arbor.

She was still suspicious. "Why weren't you there?"

"I'd just had my wisdom teeth pulled and I wasn't feeling so good." Bill ladled some noodles into his bowl. "So, what equitation events did you compete in?"

"I didn't. I didn't ride."

"What did you do?"

"I rowed at Bryn Mawr."

"Rowed! That's heavy."

"And you?"

"Chess."

"Be serious."

"I am serious. Chess." Bill was a talented athlete. In college he had been the conference wrestling champion in his weight class (light-heavyweight, 191 pound limit), and he had been a high jumper on his high school track team. But there had been pictures of him in the local papers. When the Agency created his covert identity, it decided that the bio would not include notable athletic skills.

He met her eyes, looking for rejection, but she didn't react. "Want some more noodles?"

"Not today. . . My family wanted to call me Betty. I changed it to Liz."

"Why? What's wrong with Betty?" Bill wanted to stretch. He remained square in his chair, but leaned his head to the side until his ear almost touched his shoulder.

Liz ignored the stretch but answered the question. "Betty is an antique Hollywood name. Betty Grable, Betty Hutton, Betty Boop. Betty is a name for a leggy girl in a cheesecake pose painted onto the nose of an Army airplane. With Liz, you've got Liz Taylor!"

Then Bill did the same stretch on the opposite side. He said, "You're a real movie buff. So am I. D'ya know that Lauren Bacall's real name is Betty? That's what Bogey called her."

"If you look like Bacall, the guys will come after you even if your name is Brunhilde."

Bill shrugged. "Elizabeth wouldn't be so bad."

"Sounds like a queen." She tried the head sideways exercise. She couldn't do it. "But Prince Philip calls his wife Lillibet."

Bill grimaced. "Say it ain't so."

"I'm afraid it is."

"He's cutting her down to size."

She smiled. "Silly duffer."

"What?"

"That's *Beyond the Fringe* talk."

"Who?"

"British comedy sketches—four guys from Oxford and Cambridge. Very funny."

"Never heard of 'em." Bill pushed back his chair, stood, bent at the waist, and put his palms flat on the floor.

Two young women seated at a table nearby stared and giggled. Liz didn't know them. But she admired Bill's independence and lack of self-consciousness, and she congratulated herself that she had the presence of mind to refrain from comment. He was his own man. She also noted that he was lithe. Were these stretching exercises a standard part of his first date routine? Were they designed to demonstrate flexibility that would permit unusual contortions?

She said only, "Pity."

"What?"

"More *Beyond the Fringe*.... I have an uncle who calls me Betsy. I have another who calls me Ellie."

"That's a nickname for Elinor."

"He drinks."

"You have a difficult life.... Do you plan to be a practicing anthropologist—teaching, doing research, studying the culture of some Indian tribe?"

"I'm not sure. Right now I'm more interested in contemporary American culture—why we think it's okay for us to be slaughtering people in Vietnam."

"Can you make a career out of that?"

"Probably not. But I think some self-sacrifice is necessary. It's morally required." Liz brushed her hair out of her eyes. "I don't even have a dissertation topic yet. It would take at least two more years to finish my Ph.D., and then I'd have a hard time getting a teaching job. The Vietnam war has flooded the universities with male grad students looking for a deferment. Three years from now and for decades after, there'll be thousands of Ph.D.s looking for jobs. The universities won't have places for them. So maybe I'm not really sacrificing much."

"What about doing graduate work because you love learning?"

Liz laughed. "Good luck with that!"

Bill tried a different tack. "Do you like music?"

"Yeah, sure."

"What do you like, classical?"

"No, not so much. I like music I can dance to."

"Like what?"

"I like the Beatles."

"Okay. You and several million more." Bill tried again to read her face. "The Beatles write their own stuff, so they get points for ambition and creativity. I like them too. So we have that in common."

"What kind of music do you like?"

"I used to play saxophone in a jazz band."

"Not any more?"

"I'd like to, but I'm not good enough to make a living at it."

"How do you make your living, by the way? Just by charming impressionable girls?"

"Do you want to support me?"

She laughed again.

"I'm a writer. Not that I get much money from it."

"What sort of things do you write?"

"Now I'm mostly ghost-writing."

"Oh, that's interesting. For what people?"

"Can't tell you. Professional secret. That's what it means to be a ghost."

"Okay, back to music then. What kind of jazz?"

"Trad. It was a swing band mostly. We played the standard book."

"Like what?"

"Do you know 'Body and Soul'?"

"No."

"Or 'As Time Goes By'? Humphrey Bogart and Ingrid Bergman in *Casablanca*?"

"No."

"What the hell did they do at the Upperville School on week-nights?"

"Study and read Jane Austen."

"Not James Bond?"

"Sometimes James Bond. I like Sean Connery's accent."

"So do I." Bill decided to push it a bit. "I don't suppose you've ever heard of a singer named Lee Wiley."

"No. Who is he, or she?"

"She's a great jazz singer—a singer of traditional ballads. The Gershwins, Cole Porter, Rodgers and Hart. She's still living, I think, but hasn't been heard from lately. She's the same vintage as Bing Crosby and Frank Sinatra."

"I've heard of them! They're the guys Elvis Presley and Fats Domino displaced, before the Beatles."

Bill laughed. "That's true, but give them a little more credit.

They sold millions of records, and Sinatra's still packing them in. Have you ever seen a movie called *High Society*, with Grace Kelly and Louis Armstrong?"

"No."

"Why not? It's a Bryn Mawr and Upperville School sort of movie."

"Screw you."

"Yes. Well, Crosby and Sinatra sing a duet in that, and it's a knockout. A song called 'Well, Did You Ever,' or maybe it's 'What a Swell Party This Is.' Definitely written by Cole Porter. Go see it—give yourself a treat."

"Maybe we could see it together."

"I'd like that. But first I'm going to play you a Lee Wiley record."

"When?"

"How about tonight?"

Later

Bill's apartment was conspicuously modest. There was a tiny kitchen stuck in one corner of the combination living and bedroom, plus a small bathroom. It was adequate for someone who was seldom there. It wasn't clear whether the furnishings had been left by a previous tenant or had come from Goodwill. Liz didn't ask. She had only one question.

"Where do you write?"

"At the kitchen table."

"With a pen?"

Bill laughed. "No. A portable typewriter, an Olivetti."

When she tended bar, Liz wore jeans and a plain white blouse, sometimes supplemented by a blue apron, but tonight she was wearing a nice cotton dress with a paisley print, a mixture of red, blue, and green, with yellow accents. It was from her days at Bryn Mawr and had come from Lord & Taylor.

Bill looked intently at her. "You're dressed up."

"I try."

"Me too. You want red wine or white wine?"

"Do you have any beer?"

"Beer's for the afternoon. Too late for that."

"How about scotch?"

"Nope. Red or white."

"I'll take red, thanks."

"Good choice."

"You're a gracious host."

"I try." Bill opened a bottle of California cabernet and poured two glasses. There was an awkward pause while they surveyed the seating options.

Bill said, "So, Lee Wiley. Where would you like to sit while you listen to her? I can offer the bed, the sofa, or a kitchen chair."

"Let's try the sofa."

"Suits me."

Liz sat and Bill walked the few steps to the kitchen table where there was a Webcor portable phonograph and a small pile of records. He took the top one from the pile.

"This is Lee Wiley doing 'Sugar'. It's her most famous record—not necessarily her best, but her most popular."

"Is that an LP? It doesn't look like one."

that's Michigan State in East Lansing. I'm going. With Liz. I'm not a delegate but the organization is pretty informal. I'll find out what's going on."

"Contact me on our usual schedule. I'll check on Liz Watson."

"Right. Roger, willco, and all that."

"Grow up. Don't forget that this is a job, an important one."

"Right. Got it."

Two

Hal Roberts was a graduate student in sociology, part-time, a small part. Mostly, he talked politics at the Voice bar and planned the revolution. He had spent two of his undergraduate years at Northwestern University in Evanston, Illinois, a suburb of Chicago, and the Northwestern chapter of SDS was planning a demonstration in support of peace in Vietnam. So the Ann Arbor chapter asked Hal to go to Chicago to help. They also asked Willy Feld, the new guy, to ride along.

In Evanston, Hal had arranged to meet Northwestern students at the Sherman Café, a coffee shop. The café was on a corner, just across the street from the southwest boundary of the campus. Its plate-glass windows would have permitted a full view of the diners, but it was the middle of the afternoon and there were no diners. There would be plenty of room for a private conversation.

The Northwestern students were late. Just inside the door, a sixtyish woman sat on a high stool behind a desk with a cash register and a credit card machine. When she spoke, it was clear that English was not her first language. She said, "Sit where you like."

they faced two problems—they didn't have enough men to carry heavy pieces of fence, and they were surrounded by so many students that it would have been impossible for them to move the fence through the crowd. The Evanston police were occupied directing traffic, routing commuters to the west, away from the campus. Drivers were angry but there wasn't much they could do about it.

Six campus security guards were stationed at Lunt Hall. When student demonstrators moved toward the building, the guards all went inside and locked the outside doors. Their assignment was to be on the lookout for arson and to sound the fire alarm if necessary. They had been instructed to avoid getting into fights with students. Their supervisor told them: "If students get in, to hell with the building. You get out and let it burn." The Northwestern cops were well aware that ROTC buildings had burned at other universities, and lives were more important than buildings.

Security guards went to the lower floor of Lunt, where there were ground-level windows that would be easy to crawl through or to throw a Molotov cocktail through, but there weren't enough guards to cover all of the windows. A short time later, the guards heard the glass of the front doors break, but the demonstrators were unable to get them open. There was no fire, so far.

On Sheridan Road, one of the campus police cars made the mistake of parking near the barricade. An SDS leader with a bullhorn climbed up on the roof of the car, stood, and shouted, "Peace Now! Peace Now! Peace Now!" The students took up the chant. There weren't many commuters still there to hear it.

Helen and Bill were in front of Lunt, trying to calm the more rowdy and excited students. Helen, however, was becoming bored with the peacekeeping role. She had a taste for action. She said, "Willy, let's go inside and see what's going on in there."

"There are guards inside. I saw them go in."

"They won't bother us. We're marshals. We have armbands to prove it."

"Yeah. Big deal. Official pieces of torn-up bed sheet. Why go in?"

"I want to see whether we can get into the ROTC offices."

"What'll we do there?"

"Look around. Maybe trash the place a little bit."

"A revolutionary act."

"Sure." Helen walked around to the east side of the building. Bill followed. Helen kicked one of the ground-level windows with her Red Wing boots. It broke. She pushed out the remaining glass near the latch, reached through, and opened it.

Bill said, "Nicely done. Looks like you've done that before."

"I grew up in a family of people who forget keys."

Helen climbed through the window, nimbly. Bill was larger. It would be harder for him to get through.

The guards heard the breaking glass and three of them ran down the hall toward the sound. When they reached the office, Helen was standing in the middle of the room and Bill was stuck halfway through the window.

Helen greeted the three guards with "I'm a student marshal."

The oldest guard looked at her sternly. "Oh, and what do you think you're doing?"

"Checking on things."

"What sort of things?"

erature, often dramatized as mistaken identity. Do you know 'The Scarlet Pimpernel'?"

"Sure. I'm a movie fan. Leslie Howard."

"Yes, that's right. It was also a book. What was so effective for the Scarlet Pimpernel, of course, was that he was an aristocrat and had foppish manners, so he wasn't suspected. A form of misdirection."

Bill displayed his acquaintance with old movies. "Another one like that is 'Scaramouche.' Stewart Granger. Technicolor."

"I don't know that one."

"Also misdirection. Also an aristocrat. Set in France. A nobleman disguises himself as an itinerant actor who plays a clown character in a theatrical troupe."

"Sounds like fun. The problem is that all we have to rely on is our observations. So if those observations are imperfect or deceptive or distorted, then how can we know what the reality is? Of course, we can't perceive the distortion except by reference to some reality, which we don't really know or can't be sure of. Most of the time this doesn't bother us. Is this desk in front of us real? Well, it sure feels real. I can't see why I would be wrong about that. But, in trying to evaluate whether a particular person is a friend or a foe, it's easy to see how you could be wrong. That person might want you to be wrong. So that's why trust is so difficult, so chancy."

BJ scratched his arm. Bill wondered whether that was where he injected the drug. BJ always wore long sleeves. He continued, "We can learn some things from observing animals. There are several animals, lizards and so on, that are able to change their appearance in order to hide, look more fierce, or whatever. Protective coloration. People do analogous things. Kim Philby was often reported to be charming, smart, knowledgeable. Perhaps he really was all of those things. I suppose that if you seem to be charming, then you are charming. It is a matter of perception. But clearly one of the things that permitted Philby to get away with it for so long is that people liked him and found him impressive. We now know that he was a spy. But he adopted protective coloration. He conned the establishment. We have to be careful, but we don't want to be paralyzed."

Bill found this line of inquiry uncomfortable. He changed the subject. "You said a minute ago that defectors could be recruited by ideology, that ideology could be powerful."

"I've seen it happen. I've seen conservative students here be recruited into SDS. You're a friend of Liz Watson, I believe."

"You're well-informed. But I would say it's a bit more than that."

"Okay, fine. Well, when she arrived here she was pretty conservative, but now she seems to be committed to our cause."

"You can be sure of that."

"I've seen kids go from Brooks Brothers to bomb throwers in six months. That may be because they're young. They hadn't really thought about the issues before. But once they start down that path, the enthusiasm builds. It picks up steam. And friends are important. People want to belong. Many of the people in the movement are looking for something personal. They all say they're looking for a better society of one kind or another, and that's probably true, but they also are looking for something more personal, something missing in their lives. Usually that something is purpose, a reason for being alive. I know something about that."

"You're a thoughtful man, BJ. I know you're concerned about the risk of doing harm. You just mentioned 'bomb throwers.' Maybe that was just an expression, but I'm not sure it was. Are you worried that some of those kids you mentioned may go off the deep end and hurt somebody? When I was in Chicago, the Northwestern group was talking violence. Maybe it was just talk; maybe not. But it worried me."

"Have you ever read Sorel's *Reflections on Violence*?"

"No."

"You might find it helpful. Sorel argued that occasional violence is necessary in order to purify government, rather like the way a forest fire renews a forest. Destructive renewal. But I think the question, essentially, is how much is too much? How much injustice is too much, before we will act? How many deaths in Vietnam are too many before we retaliate with real costs, personal costs? On the other hand, how much of our own violence will be too much, a disproportionate response? Violence is not always wrong. We shouldn't simply accept the immorality of the state. If we do nothing, we have to accept responsibility for that. Their bombs and bullets become ours if we acquiesce in the legitimacy of the government. So there are limits. If there are going to be bombs or bullets, then we have to direct them. We will choose our own victims instead of letting the state choose them."

"But people will still die."

"Yes, and no doubt some of those people will be us. But at least we won't have killed impoverished victims on the other side of the world who simply want to get enough to eat, a decent life. Guerrilla warfare is morally justified if the case for it is compelling. But, to be compelling, it isn't sufficient that the cause is just.

There must also be some reasonable probability of victory. Otherwise, the deaths are wasted. It will, of course, always be called terrorism, until it succeeds. There's no way to oppose a war without being accused of disrespecting the soldiers. It doesn't matter how ill-advised the war is, how brutal, how illegal, how immoral. Any arguments against the war will be called unpatriotic, failing to honor the men who are fighting and dying for their country. It also doesn't matter that the government ordered those men to fight, on threat of prosecution, that it ordered them to die. Any opposition to war, whether reasoned argument or a fist in the air, will be 'giving aid and comfort to the enemy'."

"How do you feel about protesters waving the Viet Cong flag?"

"Yeah, well, I think that's a bad move. But I confess that I don't feel much allegiance to the nation-state."

"What do you feel allegiance to?"

"That's a bigger subject. I don't think we have time for that today...but the Viet Cong flag is a matter of strategy, not principle. Our soldiers are fighting them. But we're bombing and killing Vietnamese. If you believe that our bombing is immoral and illegal, how do you express sympathy for the dead Vietnamese and their families? Waving the Viet Cong flag is a mistake, a public relations blunder, but I can understand the frustration of people who sympathize with the people we're killing."

"Philosophy is serious stuff."

"Yes, indeed it is—if that's what we've been talking about."

"Thanks very much for your advice, BJ"

"My only advice is to really, truly do what you think is right, but you may not always know for sure. Some things are uncertain."

"Doctors say 'Do no harm'."

"Yes, but they need to prescribe treatment, even though there may be side effects, and sometimes they're guessing about the outcome. An informed guess may be the best you can do. A second opinion may be a good idea, but ultimately you need to make a choice."

June, 1968, SDS national meeting

Liz owned a Volkswagen Beetle, old, red, with worn paint. It had been a gift from her parents when she graduated from Bryn Mawr. It ran. When the snow was deep in Ann Arbor, the VW sometimes sat on the street for several days before she dug it out. It was vulnerable there, but the only things that were ever stolen were the hubcaps. The car was not a promising target.

Liz drove to the Michigan State meeting. Bill didn't have a car. As they approached East Lansing, Bill spoke hesitantly. "I don't know much about SDS, about its internal politics. I might say something wrong or stupid. I don't want to embarrass myself, or you. I could be quiet most of the time, but what if someone asks me a question?"

Liz gave him some advice. It sounded as if she had given this problem some thought. "If it's a question you don't want to answer, just say something conventional but nonresponsive, like 'Thank you' or 'Not today,' or 'I don't think so,' as if you hadn't heard or hadn't understood. That makes it awkward for them to press you, and usually they'll give up. Don't say something specific like 'Unless it rains.' If it's too specific, they'll try to explain their question, make it more clear. You have to be creative. If they persist, you could try being deaf, but that's usually unpersuasive and it's inconvenient if you need to get anything done."

Bill thought she was teasing him but he wasn't sure.

The pavement was slick. They stopped talking. They needed to find the old Belmont Hotel in East Lansing. With some difficulty, they did, and Liz parked the Beetle in the hotel's lot. Police officers in uniform stood by the hotel's entrance. The lobby was filled with twenty-somethings, and Bill and Liz walked through the crowd toward the elevators. Bill was a step behind. "Where are we going? Shouldn't we be at the plenary session so that we can hear what they're saying?"

Liz turned. "Nah. That'll just be a lot of dull speeches, kids reading position papers that sound like their term papers. The real action is here and in the hallways. That's where the battles are fought."

"What battles?"

"Well, the main split now is between new radicals, younger people like us, and the old left. The old left is mostly built on the PL, the Progressive Labor Party. Just look, and you can see the difference. The PL guys have short hair, they wear work clothes, they talk about Marx and about the workers a lot. The new left is looser, less disciplined, better dressed, and a lot of them come from families like mine."

"Spoken like an anthropologist."

"Yeah, well I suppose maybe so, but just look, you'll be able to see it, even without my education."

"I'm learning." Bill put a hand on Liz's shoulder, lightly. "We could have saved money if we were sharing a room."

"That's a different kind of education." She removed his hand. "I'm not that short of cash."

"Maybe someday."

"Maybe." Liz frowned. "Have you heard of Regis Debray?"

"No. Who's he?" Again, Bill had, in fact, been exposed to Debray during his training, but he didn't want to know too much.

"He's a French philosopher who wrote a book that influenced Che Guevara. A bunch of SDS leaders have read it, or parts of it. You should know what it is. The main point is that a relatively small vanguard can lead the underclass and bring about revolution, as Che and Fidel did in Cuba. When the vanguard arms itself and organizes guerrilla action, then the working class has to choose — are they going to support the revolution or the corrupt regime?"

"That all sounds pretty risky. This isn't Cuba."

"We'll see." Liz continued walking. "In the meantime, PL has created a front group called the May 2nd Movement, a student organization. PL denies that it controls it, but it does. It's part of a PL strategy to take over SDS. That's what the politicking here is all about. Watch out for who wins the votes. PL is disciplined. Their members will fall in line."

"What are the issues? What difference does it make?

"PL is a spin-off of the Communist Party, mostly now the Chinese communists. They're always waving around Mao's little red book. Their leaders and money come from the Party. It's run by old men from the 1930s. If they win, SDS won't be led by students and it won't represent the people. It'll just be more of the old Communist line."

"So how will that be different than our agenda?"

"PL will continue what we've seen for the last thirty years. They'll run candidates and lose elections. The new left is younger, more energetic, new ideas, more radical. Real change will take radical action."

"Like what?"

"Guerrilla tactics, raids, seizures of strategic buildings."

"Violence?"

"Sure, if need be. And there probably will need to be."

"We'll have to be brave — if it isn't just theory."

"That's why we need young cadres who are willing to put their lives on the line."

Bill looked at the published program. "This afternoon there's a workshop on sabotage and explosives."

Liz shook her head. "Don't be naïve. The only reason that's there is to attract the police spies, so we can see who they are."

"Oh. " Bill hesitated. "But aren't we interested in sabotage?"

"Maybe. Time will tell." Liz smiled. "Also the workshop will create a little excitement, pizzazz, rally the troops. But I've got to run. Got to meet Hannah at the Student Center at 4:00. She's working with Steve Halliwell and Tom Bell on a position paper."

"What's it about?"

"PL is proposing a new program to unite students and workers. Hannah wants SDS to do something similar to head off the PL initiative, put the SDS name on it." Liz turned to leave. "See you later."

"So long, Liz. So long."

Liz started walking away.

Bill sang, rather tunelessly. "So long, Oolong, how long you gonna be gone?"

She turned back. "What?!"

Bill said, "Could we ever talk about anything except politics?"

Liz replied, "Like what? How about shoes and socks?"

"Have you been to Canada? Ann Arbor is getting pretty close."

"Well, when I was ten or twelve we did a family trip for the fall leaves. We went to the Algonquin Park, but it rained. Mostly I remember cream buns from a bakery in Parry Sound. I also remember staying at the Chateau Laurier in Ottawa."

"Is that the estate of one of your friends in the Brit aristocracy?"

"No, it's one of the big old railroad hotels. It was built by the Canadian Pacific, I think. It has a cavernous lobby and lots of public rooms. Lots of marble that echoes. I had metal taps on my shoes and I annoyed everyone by making clicking sounds on the floor. Not the acoustics for a soothing experience. One of the sitting rooms there has portrait photographs. They include the great one of Churchill where the photographer had taken a cigar away from him and the old man was glowering at the camera." She looked for her wallet. "The hotel is next to the locks of the Rideau Canal, a half dozen or more locks descending from the river to the lake. Stairsteps. You can watch the people on the pleasure yachts. Some are scantily dressed."

"I promise not to look."

"I also remember north of Peterborough there were fabulous petroglyphs on the granite outcroppings. Pre-Columbian, I think. They're very cool."

"Maybe we should go to Ottawa." Bill liked cities. "We could stay at the big hotel and you could put metal taps on your shoes."

"Yeah, and in another part of town there's a great Italian

restaurant owned by a woman named Stella, or Bella, or Ella. I'll find it."

"Why not? ... I haven't seen much of the metal taps side of you."

"Only on special occasions now. Anyway, we couldn't afford the Chateau Laurier."

"Maybe they would let you walk through the lobby and the halls ... How do they feel about weed in Canada?"

Liz said, "You have to be careful about that when you cross the border."

Bill agreed, "Yeah, they use it as a way to arrest guys going north to avoid the draft."

"There's a senior professor in the anthro department who's Hungarian. In the 1920s, when there was prohibition in the U. S., he used to go to Canada to pick up pint bottles of whiskey. He'd go in the wintertime and wear a sweater. He carried some extra weight, both fat and the whiskey. So he put the whiskey, a bottle or two, in his belt at the front of his pants and pulled down the sweater. When he drove through U.S. customs he'd be asked whether he had any alcohol. He'd pat his stomach and say, 'only right here.' The customs agents would laugh and say, 'That's the only place you can have it.'"

July 1, 1968, Ann Arbor

Bill walked into the Voice bar holding a local newspaper. Customers were sparse and Liz was sitting behind the bar reading a book. Bill said, "What's the book?"

"Sure is. Part of it is the Shawnee National Forest."

"Do tell. And are there really black people there?"

"Some. Not many."

"What's the economic engine in that part of the state?"

"Prisons."

"Sounds right."

"The farmland's not good."

Bill slowed. "An American story." He stopped. "Here we are at Wistful Vista." As they walked up the stairs, he turned and kissed her. "Couldn't wait."

She said, "I'm glad to hear it."

When they were inside Bill's apartment, they kissed more vigorously.

He asked the obvious question, "Do we really want something to eat right away?"

She replied, "Did you have something else in mind?"

"After that gritty movie, I think we need to be cleansed." He unbuttoned the top two buttons of her shirt. "Have you ever shared a shower?" He took his shoes off.

"I not very respectfully decline to answer." She took her shoes off.

"Oh, that's right. Of course you have. What was the Upperville School for if not a liberal education." He pulled off his shirt.

"That, sir, is a male fantasy, unsupported by fact." She took off her shirt.

"Fantasies that are unsupported by fact are always the best." He unzipped his jeans. "Come on, Babe, let's take a shower."

"Don't call me 'Babe'." She put both hands on his chest and pushed him down on the sofa.

"Would you prefer 'Sweetie'?"

"I would not." She pulled off his jeans, then removed her bra.

"How about 'Darling'?"

"Don't you dare!" She sat and pulled down her jeans.

"Okay, Sugar Lump, let's take a shower."

"Maybe Babe wouldn't be so bad." She tugged at his boxer shorts.

"Maybe the shower could come later."

Three

July 20, 1968, Ann Arbor

Liz was tending bar. An off-duty policeman was sitting on a bar stool, drinking. Bill sat at a table talking baseball with some SDS friends. The cop was about Bill's age, but had served in the Marines instead of going to college. He had not seen combat.

Liz said to the officer, "What brings you to our saloon?"

"I'm investigating."

"Investigating the booze?"

"I'm checking to make sure the whiskey isn't watered. But I'm tired of this place." He pushed a twenty-dollar bill across the bar. "What do I owe you?"

Liz pushed it back. "Your money's no good here. Professional courtesy."

"That's a genuine United States silver certificate, good money, but you people don't like the U.S.A., do you?"

"Sure we do. Some of the time."

"Or maybe you don't like police officers."

"I served you, probably too much."

The policeman turned on his bar stool and faced the room.

57

"Why aren't you lazy bastards in the Army? You're just a bunch of spoiled rich kids letting mommy and daddy pay the bills while you play at being Communists."

A slender, blond young man who was the vice president of the local SDS chapter replied. "It's not our fault that you didn't have enough brains to go to college."

The officer's face was red and his voice was loud. "Defend your country!"

Bill spoke. "Who should we defend it from? The Vietnamese didn't invade us. We invaded their country. Did you miss that part?"

"I served my country. I'm a patriot, you motherfuckers."

Liz had had enough. "You insulted my customers. You can't do that. Leave. Now."

The officer stood and put his hands on his hips. It was a John Wayne pose. "I'll leave when I feel like it."

The SDS vice president said, loudly, "Call the cops!"

Liz put her hand on the telephone. The officer reached across the bar toward her.

Bill stood. "Don't touch my girlfriend."

"Your girlfriend, huh."

"Yeah. That's right." Bill took a step toward the officer.

"I could arrest everyone in this room for smoking pot."

Bill took another step toward the cop. "Maybe so, but that would be a lot of trouble. You don't want that. Then you'd have to spend a lot of time in court, testifying and being cross-examined about why you were drinking at a bar. The time in court would keep you off the street, where the action is." Bill lowered his voice. "You were ready to leave here anyway. You don't want to have your buddies on the force be called to come and haul you out. Why don't you and I, just the two of us, go outside on the sidewalk, where we can continue this conversation in the fresh air and get away from all this smoke?"

Bill walked toward the door. The officer followed.

When they were outside, the policeman said, "She's your girl-friend. She's a terrific piece of ass."

Bill stepped close to him. "You want to be very careful, Al-bert."

"My name isn't Albert."

"It is now." Bill removed his ballcap and stuck it inside his shirt. "You and I both know that if I hit a police officer that would be aggravated assault and I could go to prison. So you can be a coward and an asshole and shoot your mouth off." Bill put his right leg a full step in front of his left. "On the other hand, if you hit me, I'm entitled to defend myself—self-defense. There are witnesses on this street, and all of them are friends of mine." Bill now spoke so softly that only the officer could hear. "You may be cocky because you're bigger than I am, but that isn't gonna mean shit if we get into it. I've handled bigger and tougher guys than you. You don't want to doubt that. So we both need to be very careful." Bill's eyes held the officer's.

The officer blinked. "Who are you?"

"A bad guy. A very bad guy who is not on any wanted list, so don't make a mistake."

The policeman said, "Bullshit," but he backed up and then walked away.

Bill went back into the bar.

Liz asked, "What happened?"

"Nothing. He got tired of the game." Bill returned to his seat.

A week later

The apartment was getting dark. The sun was going down earlier these days, and Liz was taking a late afternoon nap on the bed. Bill thought she looked beautiful resting there, peaceful, contented. "Sleeping like a baby." But he wasn't really sure what that meant—he supposed it usually meant sleeping soundly. Why did that come to mind? Liz was more beautiful than any baby and much more interesting. Besides, babies don't always sleep soundly. They're often restless, fussy—he wasn't a father but he knew that much. Although Liz was covered by a blanket, he could see the curve of her thigh. It was an aesthetic pleasure, mostly.

Bill's high school and college girlfriends were nice kids, affectionate, good-looking, but those relationships hadn't been serious. Liz was a different phenomenon. He had really liked some of the other girls, maybe at the time he had even thought he loved them. A couple of them were special, but they weren't in the same league with Liz. She was the one he wanted to be with for the rest of his life. How was that going to work with the CIA job? How did this happen? You don't fall in love, he thought, by following a plan or a checklist of reasons.

Liz stirred. She opened one eye, then the other, and smiled at him. She got up sleepily. She yawned. Bill turned on the floor lamp by the sofa.

He said, "Did you have a tough day?"

"No, I just didn't get enough sleep last night. Some guy kept me awake, fooling around."

"Pretty nice fooling, I thought."

"It was okay, I guess."

He laughed. "You know, you could get more sleep if you just moved in here. It doesn't make much sense to get out of bed in the morning and then go over to Felch Street and put on new clothes. Why not move your clothes here? Why pretend that you're still living at Felch Street? "

"I'm a respectable girl."

"Sure you are. Where do you suppose the communards think you are all night? And what makes you think they give a damn? Except maybe the guys who want to get into your pants."

"And some of the girls." Liz smiled. "Is efficiency the strongest argument you can make for my living here?"

"No, that's just an excuse. I love you, Liz, you know that. I'm crazy about you."

"Yes, I know it. I'm glad to hear you say it though." Liz sat next to Bill and kissed him on the forehead. "This apartment isn't big enough."

"We could move. I can move out any time. I could get a larger place. We could pool our money."

"I'd have to give the commune some notice, and I think I should pay my share of next month's rent. That's more or less the custom."

"That's okay. We can handle that. I can cover it for a month. No problem."

"Alright. I'll get my clothes from Felch Street tomorrow." Liz stood. "And just to celebrate this big decision, I'll make my famous spaghetti for dinner. And the starch will give you energy, and I know what that does." Liz did a little shimmy and laughed.

It was now dark outside and Bill pulled down the shades on all of the windows.

As she stood at the sink washing a plate, he came up behind her and put his arms around her waist. He pressed into her. She was still. His hands moved to her breasts. She had been expecting it. She raised her arms so that her shirt was easily pulled off. She wasn't wearing a bra—it was the 1960s after all. Her nipples were erect. She turned toward him and he unzipped her jeans. As he slid them down her hips, her underpants went with them. The kiss that followed was deep.

He formed his hand into a cup, just large enough to hold her pubic hair. "I like the feel of your fuzz, but it isn't fuzz really. It's longer and silkier than that." He smiled. "An anthropologist would probably categorize it as Protestant fuzz, Protestant silk." He stroked it. "What do you think? Is it a WASP attribute?"

"You talk too much."

"Ah. I think you're right."

Dinner was delayed.

Ann Arbor

Bill sat on a park bench next to the CIA's principal man in the Midwest. There was no one nearby. "What brings you to Ann Arbor, Tom?"

"Agency business."

"Yeah, I know there's contract research at the university, especially from the Navy."

"So I read in the newspapers." Tom wasn't giving an inch.

Bill tried again. "When the students had their referendum opposing defense research, you did a good job of turning out enough votes from the engineering school to sink it."

"All students were eligible to vote." Tom's tone was argumentative. "Since I was going to be in town, Rabbit suggested I get in touch with you. How's it going here?"

"It's going pretty well, I think. I'm getting some leads. I'm giving Rabbit regular reports. I have one very solid contact in the leadership."

"Yes, Liz Watson? I understand she's an attractive young woman."

"She is, that's true."

"How secret is the SDS?"

"Not very. They're not very sophisticated."

"They'll learn." Tom took out a cigar. With a small scissors that he kept in a leather case, pocket size, Tom clipped the end of the cigar so that it would draw. He lit it. It was his board room persona. He was only ten years older than Bill, but he valued his seniority. "It's the young who become revolutionaries, throughout history."

"Maybe that's right. Is that because they have higher ideals, they haven't been corrupted?"

Tom wanted to argue. "I suppose you could say that, but I'd put it differently. I'd say that they've not yet had enough experience of the world to make them disillusioned. Plus, not only are they young, they're usually from privileged, comfortable families.

Liz Watson is a classic case. They've never faced real barriers, never had to overcome serious obstacles. They don't know how hard it is. They can imagine a better world because they think it's possible. But that's imaginary. That's the part they don't get."

Bill was annoyed. "They have hope."

"Yes, hope but not sense. A sound rule is that we should never follow leaders who haven't experienced failure. They don't have a grasp of reality." Tom relit the cigar. He looked away from Bill, toward the trees. "A word of caution: Rabbit is paying attention." Tom drew on the cigar, then opened his mouth and the smoke drifted out. "He likes you, but he's paying attention."

"Liz isn't thoughtless. She's troubled by contradictions, aware of difficult choices. But she feels that she needs to make the choice — she isn't going to be idle, disengaged. There's anger, too. A lot of that anger comes from frustration because people won't listen. That boils over. But it isn't all emotion."

"You have to decide which team you're on, Bill. On the fence doesn't work."

Bill stood. Tom remained seated. Bill spoke quietly. "A good agent plays a role. You need to stay in character. Some ambivalence or uncertainty is okay. It adds realism. A lot of the SDSers are uncertain, to one degree or another. It's hard not to have second thoughts, and they know that."

"You need to get your head straight. You have to know why you're doing it."

"You're not a field operative, Tom. You travel around the country, smoking your cigars, holding meetings, organizing things. But you don't have to live the lie. You're an executive. I'll do my job."

"I've seen a lot more covert agents than you have, boyo. And

I've seen them screw up." Tom stood and faced Bill. "Don't think with your dick. That's a sound rule. It's in the book."

"Vulgarity doesn't suit you, Tom."

The bar again

The policeman returned to the bar. This time he was in full uniform and was cold sober. It was a quiet Tuesday afternoon. The Beatles' "All You Need Is Love" was on the jukebox. The officer removed his hat, put it on the bar, and spoke to Liz. "Where is that tough guy who was here the other night, the one who invited me outside and then walked away?"

"He isn't here, as you can see, and the people who were on the sidewalk say that you were the one who walked away."

"Well, they were all his friends." The officer paused and looked at the floor. "But I didn't come here to see him. I came to see you. I want to apologize. I'd had too much to drink and I was out of line."

Liz was polite. There was no point in making police enemies. "Don't worry about it. It happens to all of us sometimes. We all have bad days."

"I'm not a bad guy, you know. I think you might like me if you got to know me."

"Okay. Maybe so." The officer was handsome, tall, well-built. He was a better physical specimen than Willy. She smiled at him.

"I know your name is Liz. I'm Carl. Not Albert, Carl. Could I buy you dinner someday, or even just lunch, so we could have some time to talk?"

Liz considered this. A date with a police officer would be a first. She thought she should broaden her circle of acquaintances. She didn't want to be a snob. None of the girls at the Upperville School had ever dated a cop. Not at Bryn Mawr either, so far as she knew. But she was not, she realized, seriously considering going out with him. Those were just frivolous thoughts. His political views were repellent. She replied, "I'm in a relationship."

"Willy Feld told me you are his girlfriend. Is that right?"

"Well, yeah, I suppose it is."

"You don't sound sure."

"Sure enough."

"Well, think about it. You might want to reconsider. He's not a good guy."

"How do you know?"

"Take my word for it. I've seen some sons-of-bitches, and he's one of them."

"He's been nice to me."

"I'm nicer. He's bad news."

"I think you have a conflict of interest."

"Just think about it. If he gives you trouble, let me know. Ask for Carl Rivac, R, I, V, A, C."

"Eastern European."

"Yeah. Czech and Romanian mix."

As Carl walked toward the door, Liz said, "Thank you." She supposed she was simply thanking him for lust.

The dinner dance

Bill usually had a scraggly beard, three, four, five days' growth — sometimes a week or two, as his fancy struck him. Today, however, he was brushed-up. He had even been to the barber.

When he walked into the room, Liz said, "Wow! Don't you look nice."

Bill said, "Shucks, ma'am, I'll bet you say that to all the boys." Bill tightened his belt another notch. "What's the line from *Guys and Dolls*? 'When a guy smells of Vitalis and Barbasol, you can bet that he's only doin' it for some doll'?"

Liz held her nose. "I sure hope not. Soap would be enough."

"Oh, come on. Barbasol's not so bad. I kinda like it. But I don't need Vitalis. I tame this luxurious head of hair with plain water."

"I talked to my parents today." Liz gave Bill a short kiss.

"That's good. How are they?"

"They're fine. My sister is getting married."

"Oh, your sister. I forget, is she older or younger?"

"Younger. Just a year." Liz went to the refrigerator and took out a Dr. Pepper, a favorite at the Upperville School. "So my parents are excited."

"Sure. Were the two of you close?"

"I guess so. Like sisters. We weren't best buddies. We had different friends." Liz joined Bill on the sofa.

"When your younger sister gets married, does that put pressure on you?"

"Nope. Sure doesn't."

"Okay. So, are you going home for the wedding?"

"I'm going home soon, but not for the wedding. Ellen's marrying a guy from Hawaii. He's a native Hawaiian, they're going to live there, and the wedding will be in Hawaii. But there's a big reception and dinner dance scheduled in our hometown, Hiscott, and so I'm going to that. I may not have many opportunities to see Ellen in the future."

"Why not?"

"Hawaii is a long way."

"When's the dance?"

"In three weeks. I'm flying to Chicago."

"You'll have to have a fancy dress. You can't wear jeans."

"I suppose I'll have to wear the dress I wore to the Veiled Prophet's Ball. It's still in Hiscott. I think I could get into it; I haven't gained weight."

"No, you're a mere slip of a girl, as my Irish ancestors might have said."

"That's right, the Felds."

Bill laughed. "What in the hell is the Veiled Prophet Ball? Sounds spooky."

"It's a big deal in St. Louis. A big social event. There's a parade. Something like Mardi Gras, but not as raucous. And there's a ball and a big dinner."

"What or who is the Veiled Prophet?"

"Nobody knows. That's what the veil is for. It's a secret, but it's always some prominent businessman in St. Louis, a different one every year. The whole thing is organized and put on by the local business leaders." Liz made a face.

"It doesn't sound like your kind of thing."

"Not now. But maybe it was, once." She looked down. "Since we weren't from St. Louis, I couldn't be a St. Louis debutante, thank God, but we were invited because Dad is a banker and was a friend, a 'professional colleague,' of a St. Louis bank president we always called 'Uncle Fred.' I can't remember his last name. Anyhow, Uncle Fred saw to it that we were invited. I only went once."

"It's okay, I won't hold it against you."

"But I might hold it against me. It was pretty terrible of course. The V.P. had a 'court' made up of lovely young 'maidens.' (Want to bet?) Don't ask how many of them were Jewish or black. You know the answer."

"Did you have a good time?"

"My date was handsome."

"And you resisted his advances."

Liz laughed. "My father and mother were also at the ball, but we traveled in separate cars."

"Very discreet." Bill pinched Liz's knee. "Do you want company on your trip?"

"No, you're not invited."

"I see."

"I'm sorry. I didn't mean that the way it sounded. It's just that, if I bring you home to my sister's engagement party, it will look like I'm introducing you to the family and like, maybe, we're about to be engaged, too. I'm not ready for that, and I don't think you are either."

"No, that's right."

"And it would also compete with the attention to Ellen and Dan. This should be for them."

"Sure. I understand. That makes sense."

Hiscott, Illinois

The Hiscott Country Club had a room designed for this purpose. It wasn't fancy, but it would accommodate two hundred people for a heavy dinner and light dancing. Once the tables and chairs were set up, the dance floor was small. The institutional green paint, which could have been government surplus, was relieved by touches of pink, no doubt demanded by the ladies. There was a small lake on the club's property and the club was as much devoted to fishing as to golf. The fishermen seemed to have gained control of the party room: there were mounted fish hung on the walls. But Hiscott's elite was decked out for the evening, the men in tuxedos and the women in silk, organza, taffeta, brocade, the whole array. There were Hawaiian flowers on the tables and birds of paradise flanking the entrance. It was festive.

Across the room, Liz saw an old friend and classmate, Susie Hemphill. Liz had gone to school with Susie from first grade until the time came to move on to Upperville. Susie was tall and thin, as she always had been. For this occasion, she was wearing a low-cut gown. Her bony shoulders were prominent. Liz crossed the room.

"Susie, my old dancing partner!"

Susie laughed and hugged Liz. They had gone to Mrs. Smithfield's dancing school, and boys were often scarce in the student body, so there were sometimes female pairs.

Susie said, "You always wanted to lead."

"That gave you better experience. Presumably most of the men you dance with want to lead."

"They do, and some of them are pushy. You, however, were a creampuff."

"Good old dancing school. My God! Do you remember the white gloves we had to wear?"

"Sure. And the boys had to wear suits and ties. A twelve or thirteen year old boy in a suit was pretty funny. You'd have a hard time finding one in a suit today."

"And of course we towered over them. Especially you, Susie."

"The part I liked best was the instruction in how to greet people. It was all incredibly stiff and formal and routinized. Originality was not prized."

"It certainly wasn't." Liz adjusted a strap. She hadn't worn this sort of thing recently.

Susie decided that the subject had been exhausted. "I hear you're now in Michigan. What are you doing?"

"I'm in Ann Arbor, at the university. I'm a grad student in anthropology."

"How long a program is it?"

"That depends on how long it takes to write your dissertation. I'm at that stage now, so I'm really only a part-time student."

"What are you doing with the rest of your time?"

"I have a temporary job, nothing interesting. How 'bout you, Susie? Where are you now in your life?"

"I'm married. My husband, John, is in med school at Penn. He's there now, studying for exams."

"Do you plan to do graduate work?"

"No, John and I want to have children." Susie then hesitated, thinking that perhaps she had said the wrong thing. "If you lived here you could enjoy more occasions like this."

Liz said. "But you wouldn't be here. You'd be in Philadelphia."

"Yes, or wherever John gets an internship and then wherever

he decides to practice. The world is, as they say, full of opportunities."

"Yes, that's what they say."

"Have you met anyone interesting in Ann Arbor?"

"There's this one guy."

"Is he at the university?"

"No, he's a writer. Works at home."

"What does he look like?"

"He's handsome. Athletic, but not a muscle man. He's not a John Wayne type. Who does he look like? I don't know—he's good-looking but not as dreamy as Warren Beatty or Steve McQueen. Not a Hollywood type, not as smooth, his nose is slightly crooked. Maybe it was broken sometime, maybe a football injury. He's not awkward. He knows where his feet are."

"He would have been welcome at dancing class. I think you like him."

"Could be."

Then Susie's parents pulled her away to greet a cousin.

After her return

Liz had only been back for fifteen minutes. Her suitcase was still on the bed. Bill walked in and said, "How was the visit home?"

"I got to see some friends at the dance."

"That must have been fun."

"Oh, it was okay, I suppose." Liz opened the suitcase and started to unpack. The clothes looked like Hiscott. "Actually, it was weird. I don't have anything in common with them anymore.

I know they're not bad people, but they made me uncomfortable. I didn't fit in. My parents are living in the past. They want Nixon to be president. They say he would end the war. Nixon!"

"Well, would he be worse than LBJ?"

"Nixon is a bloodthirsty bastard."

"That pretty well sums it up." He put his arms around her. "I haven't had any sex in a week."

"Well, I should hope not."

July 30, 1968, Ann Arbor

Rabbit made a prearranged call to a public telephone booth at the university.

"Bill, Roger Wilkins has met with Rennie Davis, one of the organizers of the Chicago demonstrations."

"Wilkins of the NAACP?"

"Wilkins has left the NAACP to head the Community Relations Service at the Justice Department."

"What's the Community Relations Service?"

"It was part of the Civil Rights Act, intended to improve race relations, patch up local disputes, tamp down conflict. Anyway, Wilkins says that we should expect trouble at the Democratic Convention. The demonstrators' organizing committee wants permits for a march to the Amphitheater and for a rally at Soldier Field, but Mayor Daley doesn't want demonstrations and the City isn't going to grant those permits. Wilkins met with Daley, but the Mayor wasn't interested in compromise. He takes the hard line. The U.S. Attorney in Chicago is a Daley man, a ward boss. He might be inclined to help us, but he won't buck Daley. Wilkins reported all this to the Attorney General, but LBJ doesn't want to try to tell the Mayor how to run his city. There'll probably be thousands of antiwar protesters in Chicago brought by SDS, the Yippies, pacifists, the McCarthy campaign, and others. If there aren't permits, the City will try to arrest the demonstrators. You know what that means."

"What can I do?"

"See what you can find out about the plans of SDS."

August 6, 1968, Ann Arbor, the apartment

Bill said, "How are we going to get to Chicago?"

"We could drive."

"Yeah, but then we'd have to figure out what to do with the car when we get there. Parking is expensive."

"We could take the train, or there is going to be a bus." Liz busied herself in the kitchen. "Do you want pancakes?"

"Pancakes would be good." Bill joined Liz in the kitchen. "I think the bus is more fun, and probably cheaper, and we would be more plugged in to what's going on."

"Oh, I'll know what's going on, don't worry. We won't miss anything."

Bill held up a newspaper. "Tom Hayden says there'll be a big march to the Amphitheater on the 28th, the Wednesday. That's where the convention will be held."

"Did you talk to Hayden?"

"No, I read it in *New Left Notes*."

Liz said, "Some of the Voice officers are going down over the weekend before. They'll try to camp in one of the parks, but the City may chase them out."

"What will they do then?"

"Sleep on some friend's floor."

"Sounds cozy." Bill was unenthusiastic. "You and I are college graduates. Our bones are not so flexible anymore."

"Yeah. We would miss the luxury of this apartment."

"Okay, Ms. Bryn Mawr. I know the accommodations here are not up to your standard."

"Screw you."

"I wish you would."

"Not until you've finished your pancakes."

August 10, 1968, the apartment

Bill was alone. He knew that he needed to write something, maybe an assignment from one of his nonexistent ghostwriting clients. Sooner or later Liz was going to wonder why she never saw him writing.

He thought, I'd better have something in the typewriter. Maybe a piece from a story, like our drive to East Lansing. He put paper in the typewriter and began: "It was hot and George was perspiring. The open windows of the car helped, but not enough. Drops of sweat were running down his neck, but Liz was cool. She was always cool. How could she be in this weather?" He took his hands off the keys. Oh for Christ's sake! If that's the best I can do, Liz's going to know I'm a phony. This is harder than it looks. But so much crap is published, maybe my crap isn't much worse. He X'd out "Liz," typed in "Helen," and left the sheet in the typewriter.

August 12, 1968, the bar

Hal lived at the Felch Street commune, next to the room that had been Liz's. He had always hoped that she would be attracted to him. He was short and blond, just about Liz's height, and he had an assertive manner. He saw himself as a leader. An econ major, perhaps the only one in Ann Arbor SDS, he took a skeptical view of the softer social sciences, especially anthropology. This did not endear him to Liz, but he seemed unable to keep quiet about it.

As usual, the bar wasn't busy in the afternoon. Hal didn't take a seat, and he paced the room. He had Liz's full attention. "So, have you read Nap Chagnon's new book, *Yanomamo: The Fierce People?*"

Napoleon Chagnon was a University of Michigan product. He had done both his undergraduate and his graduate work there. His fieldwork among the Yanomamo, an isolated tribe in the Amazon, provided the data for his dissertation, and the book Hal referred to was a revision of the dissertation. When it was published the year before, the book made a splash, a small academic splash.

Liz replied, "Yes, of course I've read it. Nap was still in grad school when I started here, but I don't know him well."

"What do you think of it?" Hal was carrying a Coke and continuing to pace.

"The book? I think it's a fine piece of work." Liz polished the bar with a cloth. It didn't need it.

"Why does Chagnon call the Yanomamo 'the fierce people'? Are they bombing Vietnam?"

"No, but the book is about aggression. Nap thinks that an evolutionary process predisposes the Yanomamo toward violence. He observed that the men in the tribe who had killed someone fathered more children than the men who had not. So, to the extent that aggression or violent tendencies are genetic, those genes are likely to be passed on to more children. Maybe the same thing is true in other cultures, or maybe not. That is, the violent males have more kids, leading to more wars."

"Could it be that the aggressive males have more kids because they survive to breed, while the pacifists get themselves killed?"

"I think Nap was only talking about survivors. That is, killer survivors versus non-killer survivors."

"How does he know? How does he know who's killed and who hasn't, much less how many children each of them has had? Can he just waltz into a remote village in the Amazon and find all that out? He must be one hell of a detective."

"No, of course he can't just waltz in there. That's the hard part. He spent many months there."

"It sounds to me like there's a lot of guesswork involved. We have to have faith in his guesses."

"Nap counts things, like births and deaths. He isn't just making this up."

"Yeah? Do the Yanomamo have birth certificates? Or death certificates? Do they know who the father of the child was? How good is their accounting?"

"You're right. It's not as easy as copying a bunch of numbers out of a ledger or from a set of national accounts, and then plugging the numbers into a formula. Nap has to learn what information is reliable and what isn't. He has to live there for a considerable time and gain the trust of the people."

"Just like your boyfriend, Willy Feld?"

"What do you mean?"

"I don't know who Willy is. He shows up here and all of a sudden you're living with him. I don't know if we can trust him. Do you know who he is?"

"You're not jealous are you, Hal?"

August 23, 1968, Chicago

Bill took the train and arrived in Chicago on the weekend before the convention was to begin. He hoped to meet with Rabbit at the CIA's Chicago office, but they didn't have a scheduled appointment. Liz stayed behind to work at the bar on Friday and Saturday nights, the busiest times of the week. She would come on Sunday, on a bus with a group of Voice members. They all hoped to be able to sleep in the park.

On Saturday, Bill was walking on Adams Street toward the Federal Building in the South Loop when he saw Kathy Boudin about 30 feet ahead with two people he didn't know. Boudin was one of the leaders of SDS, and he had met her in East Lansing. She had been at Bryn Mawr with Liz. It was too late for him to turn around. They might have seen him already, but they wouldn't know that he was on his way to the Federal Building.

Bill greeted Boudin and was then introduced to the other two people, a young man and a young woman, both dressed in shorts.

They were all from New York City, members of the Lower East Side SDS chapter.

Boudin said, "Hi there, Willy. Are you just taking a walk?"

"No," he said, "I'm on my way to the Federal Building to pledge allegiance to the flag."

They all laughed.

"Well," Boudin said, "We've just come from there. We paid a visit to the CIA."

Bill remained stonefaced. "Does the CIA have an office in Chicago?"

Boudin nodded. "Yes, indeed it does. It's not supposed to, I think. It's supposed to spy outside the United States, so the office is secret."

"How did you find it?"

"We were told."

"Did you go in and talk to them?" Bill knew what would have happened if they had found him there. He would be looking for a new job.

"No, we couldn't get in. Of course they refused to open the door. So we painted 'CIA' on the door with red paint."

"Didn't they arrest you?"

"Well, I guess they did, sort of, but then they let us go. Federal marshals held us for about ten minutes and wouldn't let us out of the building, but then a U.S. attorney came and told the marshals to let us leave. I guess the CIA didn't want more publicity. But they took our paint."

"What office was it?" Bill looked in the window of the Berghoff's bar, absentmindedly.

"Well, we've been watching the place for a couple of days.

We've seen men coming and going, entering with keys or using the intercom. They keep changing the room number. At first, it was listed on the building directory as 'Mr. Simpson' in room 2660. Today, it said on the door '2659A GSA Gear Room.' GSA means General Services Administration. I guess the CIA provides general services."

Bill scratched an ear. "It doesn't sound like very impressive security."

Boudin agreed. "No, not very." She turned toward the lake. "See ya at the park."

Bill said, "Maybe I should go take a look. I'm curious."

Boudin shook her head. "Probably better to stay away from there now."

Bill agreed. "Maybe later."

August 24-25, 1968, Chicago, Lincoln Park

Women for Peace had twenty buses lined up to transport demonstrators to the Conrad Hilton Hotel on South Michigan Avenue where the presidential candidates were staying, but fewer than one hundred of their people showed up. Middle-class peace advocates had been scared away by the City's refusal to grant permits for demonstrations and by the talk of violence. Eventually, sixty women picketed the hotel. Police were there, and it was orderly.

Shortly after arriving at the park on Sunday afternoon, Liz and Bill were taken in hand by Howie Grossman, a PhD. candidate in physics at the University of Chicago. He handed them a jar of Vaseline. "Here, rub some of this on. It helps protect skin from Mace. If things get really bad, there could be tear gas. With gas, you can't breathe. Wrap a bandana or a T-shirt around your neck and carry a water bottle. If there's gas, wet the cloth and breathe through it."

"That's quite a welcoming speech," Liz said.

"It's practical advice. I've been through this before, when Dr. King was assassinated and the West Side was burning."

Bill thought Howie was exaggerating. "We heard that everything was peaceful last night. Why should there be trouble? All we want to do is listen to speeches, meet people like you, and advance the cause. And we heard there was going to be a music festival."

"Yeah, well the Yippies have a Detroit band lined up, but the police commander says there won't be any music. It wasn't all cool last night. There wasn't any fighting when the park was cleared, but a lot of the younger kids broke up into small groups and went running through the neighborhood, raising hell, throwing rocks, breaking windows, setting fires in trash cans. The neighbors didn't like it. Imagine that! Eleven people were arrested last night and the cops are out for blood today. Our blood. Watch out."

Liz said, "I see some priests here. I guess they want an end to the war."

"Yes, that's right, but I think they also want to try to keep peace in the park. Some of them are from the Church of Three Crosses, here in the neighborhood. We've been using the church as a meeting place for our organizers. You know who was on the other two crosses."

"Yeah," Liz and Bill both said.

"I suppose that's why we're welcome there," Howie mumbled.

"But the cops may not feel the same," Bill spoke more assertively.

"No. Maybe not," Howie agreed.

He led them toward an outdoor fireplace where the demonstrators had built a bonfire. "The organizers, and I'm one of them, want the City to pay a price for kicking us out of the park. If they are going to take away our sleeping places, then we should go into the streets and cause trouble. Maybe then the City'll wish they had let us stay. SDS and the Yippies agree on this. The National Mobilization Committee, 'the Mobe', is less tough."

At the middle of the clearing, near the fire, Liz found Hannah Meyer and greeted her.

"Hi, Hannah, what's doin'?"

"Not much, Liz, I'm sorry to say. We don't have enough troops. The Mobe thought we could force the city to cooperate. Rennie Davis, David Dellinger, and Tom Hayden said that there would be a hundred thousand protesters in the parks."

Liz asked, "How many do we have?"

"Maybe two thousand. Not nearly enough. With a hundred thousand, Mobe planned that it would be impossible for the City to clear us all out. Too many police or soldiers would be required. And the mass of demonstrators would only move somewhere else. There's no place big enough to hold that many. But, with two thousand or so protesters, we can be ordered to disperse and the National Guard could handle any resistance."

"So what should we do?"

"Improvise." Hannah smiled. "We can always cause trouble."

Despite the police commander's ban on music, a band began

playing at four p.m. The Yippies had advertised it as The Festival of Life. The park's usual Sunday visitors liked the music, but the City wouldn't let the Yippies use their flatbed truck as a stage, so the band set up on the grass and people just gathered around. Bill and Liz were only twenty yards from the band, but they couldn't see anything except the heads of the people in front of them. The crowd became angry and restless. People at the back who were trying to get a better view pushed. Bill said to Liz, "This isn't going to help keep the crowd calm and quiet."

Then the electricity went off. The protesters didn't know why. Two boys standing next to Bill and Liz said the City turned it off. But it might have been a short circuit. In any event, the band's amplifiers went dead and the music stopped.

Abbie Hoffman, the Yippie leader, had a bullhorn. He told the crowd that the police wouldn't let the band use the truck as a stage, but then he recruited a Yippie known as "Super Joel" to drive the truck into the middle of the crowd. People jumped up on it. Super Joel led the crowd in taunts of the police—mostly "Pigs eat shit!"

Police moved in and the crowd surged toward the police. "Pigs eat shit!" intensified. In return, cops shouted at the demonstrators, calling them "fags." Liz was nervous. She said, "This is really nasty. "

Bill replied, "Yeah, get ready to move, quickly, if this breaks loose."

Hoffman, with the bullhorn, announced that the music festival was over, something that was already apparent.

As the sun went down and the air began to cool, other bonfires appeared in the park. Police crews extinguished them, but demonstrators rebuilt the fires, sometimes fighting police in the process. Bill and Liz stayed out of the way. They consulted Hannah about strategy, specifically about whether it was wise to fight the police.

Hannah was prepared for the question. "The SDS leadership discussed this. We're getting great television coverage. All the networks are here to cover the Democratic Convention. Walter Cronkite, Chet Huntley and David Brinkley are in town, and even Norman Mailer is here writing about it all for a magazine. TV cameras everywhere. We could have hundreds of marches and rallies and demonstrations, give a thousand speeches, and we wouldn't get as much attention, as much coverage as we have this week. This is our chance!"

Bill asked, "How do we take advantage of it?"

"There are two ways to play it. One is we can try to persuade the voters by making the arguments and making our case. We can explain the reasons why the war is wrong. That'll put people to sleep. The other is we can piss off the Chicago cops and get them to overreact. Let them beat us up while everybody is watching. Let them use billy clubs and Mace and tear gas to stop free speech. Show the world how much Chicago values the Constitution. We'll get bruised, but we'll win. Bruises heal."

It played out as she expected—except that the electorate did not side with the demonstrators.

News about confrontations with police traveled through the park. When one police squad chose to surround the public restrooms, perhaps preferring urination in the trees, the police shortly found themselves facing angry kids, a mob of them. Other demonstrators, hearing the commotion, were attracted to the area. Soon there were several hundred students of varying ages, many of them locals, shouting: "Motherfuckers!," "Oink, oink," and "Shithead." At first the cops did not react. But then they did. They charged the crowd, swinging their batons. Most of the kids ran, the ones who were quick enough. Those who weren't quick got hurt. By the time Liz and Bill heard about this, it was too late for them to join the restroom fight. They found it difficult to sort out all of the confusion and rumors.

At eleven p.m., right on schedule, a line of police, what the commanding officers called a "skirmish line," moved into the park to clear it. But some of the demonstrators were determined to stay and met the police in a large parking lot near the western border of the park. Bill and Liz were at the far north end of the assembled protesters, away from the center of the action. For a few minutes that seemed much longer, the two contending forces stood face-to-face. The police were outnumbered by about ten to one, perhaps twenty police to two hundred demonstrators, mostly kids. Then the police moved forward.

Bill asked Liz, "How deep do we want to get involved in this? The police are going to club their way into the park. People will get hurt."

She replied, "We should help our brothers and sisters."

He did his neck-stretch move and said, "Well, sure, but the question is how to do that. We can't help much from a hospital bed."

Liz moved closer to the center of the action and Bill followed. The skirmish line broke apart as individual cops clubbed individual kids. Protesters shouted, "Hell no, we won't go!" Police used Mace. Then tear gas. Bill and Liz were far enough away to avoid the gas. The breeze was blowing in the other direction. The gas was already drifting toward neighborhood houses on the west side of the street. The police line dissolved. Protesters ran into the neighborhood. Cops chased them. Bill and Liz stayed in the park.

Bill wanted to avoid trouble, but he didn't want to appear to be a coward. His credibility within SDS was essential, and Liz would expect him to act. The SDS leaders, however, had told the members to leave the park peacefully, so he and Liz headed toward the residence of the Cardinal of the Chicago Archdiocese, just south of the park, across North Avenue. But the police were not letting people leave the park in that direction. The City wanted to protect the Cardinal. When Liz reached the boundary, a cop blocked her path. She told him, "We just want to leave." But an informant had told the City that the SDS plan was to form groups after leaving the park and then roam through the streets. A more accurate description of SDS plans is that there were many of them. In any event, the police were determined to stop Liz and Bill.

The policeman, taller and heavier than Bill, pushed Liz. She stumbled and fell to the ground. Bill asked her whether she was hurt. She said, "No." Bill then stepped directly in front of the cop and said, "Sonofabitch!" The officer swung his baton. Bill ducked under the baton, head-butted the cop, and broke the cop's nose. As Bill's head was next to the policeman's ear, Bill said, "Fall down. Take a dive so I don't have to hurt you more." The cop said, "Fuck you" and perhaps something else that Bill couldn't understand because the words were garbled by blood from the officer's nose. The cop tried to swing his baton at Bill's groin, but

Bill grabbed the baton arm with both hands, about two or three inches above the wrist, pivoted quickly, and dislocated the arm. The cop was out of action.

Liz said, "How did you do that?"

"Just lucky, I guess."

They took advantage of the opportunity to leave, a wise decision. Howie had offered to let them stay at his apartment in Hyde Park, the University of Chicago neighborhood, and they accepted his hospitality. Liz slept on the sofa and Bill in his sleeping bag on the floor.

Fighting between police and demonstrators, in the park and on the streets, continued until two a.m. The police were in no mood to be lenient. No one was exempt—a priest wearing a clerical collar was clubbed. His skull was fractured. Mobile TV crews roamed the park. Their lights could be seen from a distance. Both demonstrators and police were filmed when they would rather not have been, but the police were able to do something about this. They used their batons on the reporters and the cameras. A delegation of newspaper and broadcast executives complained to the mayor and demanded a meeting with the superintendent of police. Not much came of it. Police still hit reporters and smashed cameras. This resulted in unfavorable coverage on the next day's news, developments Liz and Bill followed on TV.

August 27-28, 1968

Lincoln Park, where the SDS demonstrators congregated, is north of downtown. Mobe and the Yippies preferred Grant Park, directly across the street from the Michigan Avenue hotels where most of the convention delegates were staying. Howie Grossman explained the difference. "The police have been told to protect the delegates, and the City says that means keeping demonstrators away from them. Of course, keeping them away also keeps the peace marchers from communicating with the delegates, which suits Daley fine. So the Mobe people are just across the street from the hotel, as close as they can get."

Bill asked, "What about the Yippies?"

"Oh, they just want to smoke dope and not get hurt," Howie said. "They figure the cops will be gentler, more careful, downtown on Michigan Avenue. The cops want to avoid crap in full view of the TV cameras assembled for coverage of the convention, or the Yippies hope they do."

By Tuesday night, the number of demonstrators had increased. Many of them had come to Chicago to take part in the Mobe's march to the Amphitheater, where the convention was held. The march, intended to support a proposed "peace plank" in the Democratic Party's platform, was scheduled for Wednesday afternoon, but the City had refused to grant a permit for the march and the mayor would not let the protesters get near the Chicago Amphitheater.

Some of the people in Lincoln Park were supporters of SDS and other political groups, but many were simply local teenagers looking for action. Although most of the protesters were white, a large number of blacks were present on Tuesday because Bobby Seale, the national chairman of the Black Panther Party, was scheduled to speak.

He spoke in the early evening. He had much to say about

guns and about the desirability, the inevitability, of using them. He used the word "shoot" repeatedly. Liz was somewhat shocked by the explicit violence of the speech, but Bill thought that it was ingenious. It was a jumble of words, sufficiently ambiguous and incoherent to provide a legal defense to a charge of incitement, and it was effective. The rhetoric was intended to be incendiary, and it was. It fired up the crowd, especially the young blacks.

Later that night, a group of clergymen carried an eight-foot tall cross into the park and set it up in a small clearing where a number of them made speeches and offered prayers. Protesters huddled around the cross. It was then well after the eleven p.m. curfew time. Suddenly, heavy tear gas canisters broke through the branches of the surrounding oak trees and landed in the middle of the crowd, near the cross. One of the cans narrowly missed Bill. He shouted, "Christ! If one of those hits someone in the head, it'll kill him." Another man yelled, "It's a bombing campaign, just like Vietnam. We're at war." It wasn't a joke. The canisters then released the gas. People screamed, when they could. Bill and Liz coughed and choked and didn't have enough breath to scream. They joined hands to lead each other out of the gas. The police had found a weapon that worked.

Kids once again took to the streets. Those who had tools began pulling up asphalt pavement, breaking it into chunks, and distributing the rocks to their friends. Pieces of pavement were thrown at the police cars driving through the streets and the park. The crowd demolished at least a dozen of them. Mobs of kids chased down lone cops, and threw rocks and bricks at them. Police fired shots into the air.

Bill and Liz left Lincoln Park to escape the tear gas and went straight to Howie Grossman's apartment to sleep. They later heard that in Grant Park the demonstrators were permitted to spend the night. The curfew was waived there. By two a.m., the police in Grant Park had been on duty for fourteen hours, but the National Guard was standing by and at three a.m. it arrived, six hundred soldiers in full battle gear, with fixed bayonets. Most carried M-1 rifles; some had shotguns. The guns were probably not loaded, but ammunition was readily available.

Nearly one hundred arrests were made that night. Seven policemen were injured, but the police had the better, more effective weapons. More than sixty protesters required medical attention. By 1:30 a.m., Lincoln Park was quiet. There was still tear gas in the air. The few remaining protesters held wet rags, T-shirts, and the occasional handkerchief over their noses and mouths. The police had gas masks.

August 28, 1968, Wednesday

Howie had to go the emergency room for treatment of a rib cracked by a policeman's baton. He explained to Liz and Bill that it was a simple matter of physics, something about mass and velocity. The medics at the hospital taped him up and told him to rest for a few days. He wanted to walk in the Mobe's march, but the rib hurt and he decided to stay home. Liz and Bill got a ride downtown with some U of C students.

Grant Park is between Michigan Avenue and Lake Shore Drive, which runs north and south along the lakefront. Most of the park is open land with grass, but there are a few areas with trees. A bandshell was at the south end of the park, not far from the Conrad Hilton across the Avenue, and the crowd assembled at the bandshell was visible from the windows of the upper floors of the hotel. That's why the Mobe wanted to hold the rally there. Delegates would see it. Mobe had a permit for the rally, and it was not expecting trouble with that, but the march to the Amphitheater would be another matter.

Shortly after Liz and Bill arrived at the bandshell, perhaps fifteen minutes after their arrival, Liz grabbed Bill by the arm. "Willy, turn around, face the lake."

Bill did as he was told, but asked, "Why?"

"The cop from the other night, from Lincoln Park, is here. He's not in uniform, and he has a bandage taped to the middle of his face, and his arm is in a sling. It's the same guy. He's twenty or thirty yards away, looking in our direction."

"Did he recognize me?"

"I don't think he could see your face. And you were dressed differently the other night. You had on your red jacket then. But he was looking at us. He was staring at me hard."

"Let's move over there behind that Jeep."

The National Guard was using Jeeps converted into "people dozers." A frame made of angle iron was welded to the front of the Jeep and barbed wire was strung across the frame. When Jeeps like this were driven toward a crowd, the people would move back.

From cover behind the Jeep, Bill got a look at the cop. "Yeah. That's him. He's making his way through the crowd and looking around. I don't think he knows where we are."

Liz took charge: "You should leave. He's hunting for you. I

don't think he got a good look at me the other night. It was dark, and I didn't hit him, but he sure saw you. He wants to bust you."

"Yeah. I think you're right. . . . Maybe you should leave too."

"No. I want to stay. He doesn't have anything on me, and I'll be less conspicuous if I'm not with you."

"Okay, but be careful. Ask BJ if you can borrow his straw hat. Explain why. He'll be sympathetic. Push your hair up under the hat if you can."

"Yeah, good idea. You make yourself scarce. I'll meet you back at Howie's place tonight."

Bill left the park immediately. Then he had to wait. That was uncomfortable because he didn't know what was going on. He went to Howie Grossman's apartment, or he tried to, but it wasn't easy. He took the "El" to the South Side, but the train stop was too far west. It let him out on Garfield Boulevard, west of Garfield Park, a long walk from the University and Howie's place. Bill was eager to get to a TV set so that he could find out what was happening in Grant Park. He was worried about Liz, and he was also conscious that he wasn't gathering much information about SDS activity or strategy at this point. He was, in effect, out of action. All he would be able to tell Rabbit was what anyone could see on television.

When he reached Howie's, all three of the major networks were showing armed soldiers in full battle gear on Michigan Avenue in front of the Hilton, just across from Grant Park. The people dozers were on the street, driving toward the protesters. It looked like the battle of Algiers. Worse than Selma! Young people—students, they looked like—were being beaten by police with truncheons. The kids were being hurt, but not as badly as they would be if they were shot by the soldiers. Where was Liz? He flipped the channels to try to catch a glimpse of her. He didn't see her. It wasn't reassuring. He paced the floor. He could only wait.

When Liz got to Howie's apartment six hours later, Bill said, "I've been watching TV, watching the cops beat up people for the viewing pleasure of the national audience. I was afraid you'd get hurt."

Liz sat down in an upholstered chair. She was tired, but she looked triumphant and she made a report. "The permit for a peace rally at the bandshell didn't mean much. The first thing that happened was the flag battle. There was an American flag on a pole. One of our people hauled it down and put up something else. Somebody said that what went up was another flag, and somebody else said that it was an old pair of blue jeans. Maybe some guy lost his pants. Anyhow, this pissed off the police, plenty. A group of them attacked, swinging their clubs. People started getting their heads cracked, bleeding. Many of the Mobe kids were pacifists. They only wanted peace.

"Rennie Davis tried to speak to calm the crowd. He had a bullhorn, but the cops clubbed him on the head and knocked him out. He had a three-inch cut in his scalp. The cops knew who Davis was; they targeted him. It wasn't a mistake. I tried to run away, but we were trapped against the bandshell, and the City had closed the bridges so we couldn't get into the Loop, and the bridges were the only way out of the park. There were National Guard soldiers with machine guns at the bridges—mounted machine guns!

"The cops had us held captive and they beat the crap out of us.

But they didn't hit me." Liz went to the refrigerator and got a Coke. "It wasn't about preserving order or containing a demonstration. It was all about punishment, vengeance. We couldn't go anywhere. The cops acted like they were nuts. They took off their name badges and even tore off their unit insignia so they couldn't be identified. They knew damn well that what they were doing was illegal.

"Some of our people—a mixture of SDS and Yippies, with maybe some local high school kids—got to one of the farther north bridges before the National Guard troops, and they reached Michigan Avenue just as the mule train of the Southern Christian Leadership Conference was going by. The mule train had a permit for a march, or maybe for a parade. So our people joined the mule train, until the cops put a stop to it.

"The cops, or maybe the Guard, used tear gas in the park and the wind blew the gas across the street into the Hilton's air conditioning. Guests of the hotel started leaving to avoid the gas. Then it seemed like the cops were beating everybody, including spectators on the sidewalk. You maybe saw that on TV. The cameras were set up right in front of the Hilton, and the networks taped a lot of it. Cops pushed one group of people through the plate glass window of the Hilton's bar. People were cut and bleeding. I don't think the City could have messed up much worse."

Liz sighed. "Cops are recruited from the same talent pool as strong-arm criminals. The difference is that the public buys uniforms for cops, buys their work clothes so they don't get blood on their own shirts and pants and boots. The Chicago police are thugs. Don't ever trust those sons-of-bitches."

Bill spoke softly. "The City didn't want a rampage on the streets of the Loop. There are too many restaurants there, too much money, also too many politicians. The Lincoln Park troubles scared them. Most of the kids running out into the streets to raise hell aren't SDS, and they aren't peace marchers. They're just Chicago hoods from the wrong side of town who want to have fun. They don't give a damn about peace in Vietnam or anywhere else. They aren't interested in politics. They just want to break into cars, maybe find something to steal, break some windows, piss off the cops. Hoffman and Rubin use the Chicago gangs to make it look like Yippie has more troops. But those kids are not on our side, Liz. They don't want what you and I want. What good is it to break windows and steal from cars? What will that accomplish? Is it going to make politicians want an end to the war?"

Liz was thinking about something else. "Police work tends to be an inherited occupation. Lots of cops have fathers who were cops—a family tradition. I wonder whether the Chicago police are like the Yanomamo, if there's an inherited disposition toward violence. Certainly their culture encourages it, endorses it. Maybe the more aggressive cops have more kids."

"Always the anthropologist."

September 20, 1968, Ann Arbor

Bill went to a phone booth at the post office to receive a prearranged call from Rabbit.

"Bill, the Chicago Police have a warrant for the arrest of one Willy Feld on a charge of felonious assault. It appears that Feld broke the nose and dislocated the arm of a Chicago policeman. It sounds like an unfortunate misunderstanding."

"Yeah. It was a bad scene. I wonder where they got the name, who they got it from."

"That's a good question. Maybe we have a problem. But the warrant says 'address unknown,' so far. I'm going to try to see that the paperwork gets misplaced, but behave yourself. Keep a low profile."

"I will. You saw the Chicago police. The cop knocked Liz down. He pushed her. She says she stumbled, but she was on the ground. The cops were nuts. They were provoked, but they were nuts."

Rabbit put the point in more professional terms. "Command and control completely broke down. Just be careful, Bill. You have to maintain your cover, of course, but don't use more force than necessary."

"I'll try to use good judgment."

"Can't ask for more."

Bill said, "The SDS leadership was pleased with Chicago. They think it showed the weakness of the government."

Rabbit had data. "A poll done by the Survey Research Center found that barely more than ten percent of white respondents thought the Chicago police used too much force, and a quarter of them thought the police had not used enough force."

Bill said, "Yeah, the Survey Research Center is a part of U of M. That research was done here in Ann Arbor. I have the report right in front of me. You're correct about the way the whites felt, but blacks' responses were very different. Sixty-three percent of blacks thought too much force was used, and that went up to eighty-two percent among college-educated blacks. The Chicago violence produced a huge racial split. That's why SDS is going to try for an alliance with the black leadership, Dr. King's successors. Or worse, with the Black Panther Party. I reported on Bobby Seale's speech in Lincoln Park. I'm sure you remember."

"Yes, I do. But a Harris poll done during the convention found that less than a quarter of all Americans thought we should stop bombing Vietnam. So take your choice. Should we let public opinion decide what's right? Or should we let radical groups decide? Just be careful, Bill."

Photographs taken in Chicago in August of 1968 during the Democratic National Convention. (Photos by Bill Hood)

Four

September 24, 1968, University of Michigan

Two hundred students, along with a handful of political activists such as Liz and Bill, were packed into a smoky classroom at the university. It was the new academic year's first meeting of the SDS chapter (formerly Voice). There was a feeling of energy and anticipation. Everyone knew what had happened in Chicago the month before. As the students milled about looking for chairs, Bill turned to Liz, "Does anyone know how to sing the 'Internationale'?"

"No," she said, quietly.

"Okay, how about the 'Marseillaise'? It's a better song."

Hal Roberts heard him. "Don't be an asshole."

Bill said, "Too late to change now."

The meeting started. It was all pretty routine for fifteen minutes or so, with committee reports and desultory, stale accounts of the events at the Democratic convention. When the meeting turned to proposed action concerning the presidential election, however, discussion became heated. There was some support for the view that the nominations of both of the major party candidates had been engineered by a conspiracy. One student called the election a "fraud." Another tried to argue in favor of Hubert Humphrey, but he was drowned out by shouts of "Dump the Hump!" Many students thought that there should be some expression of outrage.

The elected leaders of the chapter, all of them undergraduates, proposed a program of "political education," including the distribution of leaflets listing the evils of both Humphrey and Nixon. They didn't bother to mention George Wallace, running as a third party candidate opposed to racial integration.

Jim Mellor stood and said, loudly, "This is bullshit." Mellor was new to the campus and a bit older, perhaps in his late twenties. He was a blond giant, six feet four inches tall, two hundred and twenty-five pounds, and there didn't appear to be any fat on him. He was forceful, and was well read in Marxist theory. "This isn't the time for education. This is the time for action! SDS tried last year to educate the University. You tried to tell people about the war-mongering here on campus at the Institute for Defense Analysis, bought and paid for by the Defense Department. You even had buttons made with 'Go Michigan, Beat Thailand!' Cute! But not very serious. And what did it get you? You were finally permitted to hold a referendum on whether defense research should be kicked off campus. And what happened? You lost! Badly. Your education campaign didn't work. It's too late for more education now. We need to kick this institution in the balls! We were kicked in the balls in Chicago. It's time to kick back." He sat down to loud applause.

The chapter leadership made a game attempt to return to the agenda that had been planned for the meeting, but it was too late.

They suggested picketing the ROTC office on campus. This was met with foot stomping and shouts of "Burn it down!"

Bill then stood and proposed that SDS close down the University, as had been done at Columbia. He said they should occupy the administration building, including the president's office, until their demands were met. He was asked what demands he had in mind.

Bill replied, "Here are a few of them. Number one: let's find out what stocks are in the U of M endowment fund. Does the school have an investment in the continuation of the war? Is Dow Chemical on the list? We should demand that the University stop profiting from the war. Number two: Kick the ROTC off campus. It's outrageous that this school gives college credit for courses teaching how to organize an invasion of another country. At West Point, maybe. I admit, the Normandy invasion was a good thing. So maybe at West Point, but not here. Number three: fly all University flags at half-staff until the Vietnam War ends, in honor of all the people dying there. Number four, disarm the campus cops. Those clowns should not be carrying guns. Their only purpose is to intimidate us. So, that's a start on a list of demands. There could be more." Bill sat. There were cheers of "Right on!" and "Way to go, Willy." Jim Mellor shook Bill's hand.

Liz asked Bill, "Did you prepare that speech, or did you just make it up as you went along?"

He said, "I had some ideas in mind."

September 30, 1968, phone call

One of the phone booths that Bill used was in the U of M gym. Bill went to the gym often and his presence there did not attract attention. The phone was seldom used.

"The first SDS meeting of the fall term was held a few days ago," he told Rabbit. "There's trouble brewing. I even made a speech to try to head off worse trouble. As a result, we may organize a sit-in at the university president's office. That won't do much harm. It's better than having campus buildings burned, like at Columbia."

"Bill, your job is to collect information. You aren't there to make SDS policy. If you get word that someone is going to be killed or seriously injured, then we alert the local authorities, but otherwise you shouldn't interfere. Keep a low profile."

"If I'm going to have access to the information you want, I have to play a role, I can't just be a cipher. I have to have some discretion, some room to maneuver."

"Alright, use your judgment, but try to keep it cool. Mostly watch."

"Thanks. At the meeting there was debate about tactics. The elected leaders wanted to continue with their program of political education—printing leaflets, making speeches, holding protest marches, recruiting faculty to do radical seminars. But there's now another group, mostly led by older guys who aren't students, who are pushing for more violent tactics. It's pretty clear that this new group is trying to take over the U of M chapter. They had a lot of support. The kids are fired-up as a result of the police in Chicago. They saw that on TV, were sorry to miss the action, and now they're eager to cause trouble so that they can show how brave they are."

"Sounds juvenile."

"Some of it is, certainly, but some is also genuine outrage at the Chicago cops."

"Who are the players in this new group?"

"One is Billy Bissell. His daddy is the chairman of the electric company in Chicago. Another is a little bulldog named Hal Roberts—obnoxious, barks a lot, aggressive, but not dumb. Then there's Jim Mellor. He's older, but I don't think he's a graduate student. There are people on the campus or who live nearby and who just seem to be around. Mellor is one of them. I don't know where he came from. He's an effective advocate, persuasive, but some of the SDS leaders suspect he's a plant. I don't know whether he is or not, and I don't want to know, but you should be aware that's being said."

"Don't get in Mellor's way. That doesn't mean he's our man—he isn't—but we can't get in his way. Enough said. You may believe whatever you wish, but stay out of his way."

"Okay. Unfortunately, Liz is way too tight with this new group. She seems to think they're cool. I think they're bad news."

"You'll have to let Liz figure that out."

Bill decided to avoid further discussion of Liz. "The SDS action in Chicago was unpopular with the general public, but it was sure good for recruiting students to the cause. The chapter meetings on most campuses this fall have been mobbed with new members."

Rabbit sighed. "Public opinion is fickle. The protest against the war wasn't popular, but the war isn't popular either. Since the

Tet Offensive, when our casualties increased to 500 dead Americans per week, opinion has shifted against the war. The president is worried, as he should be. A short time ago, only a quarter of our citizens thought that it was a mistake to send troops to Vietnam. Now, a majority do. The American people don't like losing, or maybe they just don't like to see their kids being killed without the country getting anything for it."

As Bill left the phone booth, Hal Roberts walked by. Bill wondered whether Hal had been tailing him. Hal said, "Urgent telephone business?"

Bill replied, "My mother likes to know I'm still alive." Bill made a mental note that he shouldn't use that phone booth again.

November 4, 1968, University of Michigan

The trees were bare, the leaves had all been raked, and it was a bright, clear November day. U of M football weather. Jim Mellor and Bill Burke (as Willy Feld) waited outside the administration building for the students who would occupy the president's office. A university police car parked nearby had two officers in it, watching.

Mellor said, "Willy, should we plan a rally for when the election results come in, maybe a protest march?"

Bill shrugged. "What do we protest? We don't want either Nixon or Humphrey. I suppose we could protest no matter which one wins, but it seems kinda weird that we would be protesting that someone won, protesting that there's actually gonna be a president."

"Yeah. You're right. The election is irrelevant for us. It's beside the point. They're both bad."

Bill looked around. "Where are all the students who were supposed to be here? We can't take over the building if we've only got a handful of students."

"It's early yet. We passed the word. I think they'll be here."

"I hope so. Our demands aren't going to mean much if we don't have any bargaining power."

Mellor said, "Taking over administration buildings hasn't worked too well or been too popular. Look at Columbia and the University of Chicago. The paychecks of the university's employees get delayed, so faculty and staff are angry, and students who need transcripts in order to apply for jobs can't get them, so they're pissed off. My vote is that we occupy only the president's office, where nothing much gets done anyway, and that we only stay for a few hours, not overnight."

It had been Bill's project. He felt a need to defend it. "But, if we do that, there's no chance that the university will agree to our list of demands."

Mellor was practical. "They weren't going to anyway. The importance of the demands was to get publicity, provide the media with a list of grievances. The trustees are never going to agree to disclose the investment portfolio or get rid of Defense Department research funds—there's too much money at stake—but they might agree to fly flags at half-staff and maybe disarm the campus cops. A gesture."

Bill acquiesced. "I think we should stay in the building long enough to make the cops carry us out the door. That would get pictures in the newspapers, which would have some recruitment value."

"I agree. We shouldn't simply walk away. I'm willing to be carried if they have guys big enough to lift me."

"Me, too. Of course, that means we'll probably also be arrested. I have to be careful. Chicago has a warrant out for my arrest because of a tussle with a cop in Lincoln Park."

"Yeah. I heard you broke a cop's nose."

"An unfortunate accident. Don't forget that I also dislocated his arm."

Mellor laughed. "I heard that, too. You're a clever fellow."

"Except that Chicago put out a warrant." Bill hoped that Rabbit had solved that problem, but he hadn't heard where it stood.

"What happens if you get arrested here?" Mellor grabbed Bill by a shoulder, maybe a gesture of solidarity or maybe an imitation of a police move.

"If I'm arrested here and the warrant shows up, they wouldn't let me go. They'd hold me and tell the Chicago police to come get me."

"So what can you do?"

"I need to hope that they won't identify me. I'll give them a phony name. My pockets are empty. I've removed everything except a couple of quarters."

"Will the empty pockets stop them from investigating?"

"No."

At 11 a.m., Jim and Bill decided that they had waited long enough. About 200 to 300 students had assembled. The U of M student population was 20,000. So it wasn't a big turnout, but even if the campus police managed to mobilize thirty officers, there would be enough students to surround the police and enter the building. The cops wouldn't want to fight with students. It wasn't worth it. But if the students refused to leave the building by the end of the day, the Ann Arbor city police would be called in.

By noon, more than two hundred students had succeeded in entering the building, and about fifteen were in the president's office, one sitting in his chair. The president had gone home as soon as students started congregating outside. Jim Mellor and three big guys were guarding the front door. Liz and Bill were both in the president's office.

At 5:00 pm, Ann Arbor police cars started to arrive. Bill watched from the window. One of the cops getting out of the second car looked familiar. Bill took another look and realized that it was Carl Rivac.

Bill turned to Liz and spoke softly. "There's a problem. Carl Rivac is here, the cop from the bar. He knows who I am."

"So?" Liz was in a militant mood.

"There's a warrant out on me from Chicago. If Rivac identifies me, they'll lock me up and throw away the key. I've got to leave."

"Okay, but I'm staying." Liz kissed him on the forehead. "I'll see you at home."

Bill went down the stairs and out the back door.

A short time later the police announced on a bullhorn that all students were required to be out of the building within ten minutes. If they were not, they would be arrested.

Liz refused to leave. She was now in the president's chair, but only briefly. Half an hour later, she was carried out by Ann Arbor police. She struggled. When they reached the front door, she tried to get away, but didn't succeed. The officer had Liz's arm pinned behind her. "You're going to be charged with disorderly conduct and resisting arrest. You can spend some time cooling off."

Carl Rivac, who had been in the process of arresting another demonstrator ten feet away, said to the officer, "I'll trade you. You take my felon and I'll take yours. I've had some contact with her before."

The officer holding Liz looked puzzled, but he shrugged and agreed. The important thing was to clear the area.

Carl held Liz's arm with a firm grip but it was no longer pinned behind her. "Do you remember me?"

"Sure, Carl. You're the cop who came to the bar. And your name badge reminds me that your last name is Rivac, R-I-V-A-C."

"I hate to see you here, involved in this kind of crap. You're going to have to get into the squad car with me."

"Am I ordered to?"

"Yeah."

"Are we going for that cup of coffee now?"

"Don't be a wiseass." The squad car was parked on the sidewalk in front of the building. "I'm going to push your head down so you don't bump it when you get into the back seat. You're going to be locked in there."

"Will more prisoners be put in with me?"

"No, I don't think so. We're going to take a little ride."

"Where to?"

"Be quiet. Behave yourself for a change. This isn't intended to be fun."

The car smelled of the sweat of other prisoners, or maybe it was just the sweat of the police officers. The front seats were separated from the back by a barrier of reinforced glass, but there was an intercom. Carl switched it on. He started the car and headed toward the station. When he got to Felch Street, however, he took an unexpected turn.

Liz said, apprehensively, "Where are we going?"

"This is your lucky day, Liz. You got the 'Get Out of Jail Free' card. I didn't see you do anything, so I can't sign a complaint against you. I'm going to let you go."

"No favors, Carl."

"No, no favors." He drove to the corner, stopped, unlocked the back doors, and let Liz out. The apartment was only short walk away.

"Thank you," she said.

He replied, "I won't do this again."

Thanksgiving 1968, Ann Arbor

Liz and Bill sat at the kitchen table waiting for the bread in the toaster to brown.

He spoke. "You were restless last night."

"Mmm hmmm."

"I was aware that you were moving around."

"I woke up at two and couldn't go back to sleep."

"What was wrong?"

"The world. The government. Evil. Chicago. What to do about it."

"That's a big subject."

"Yeah. I couldn't stop thinking about it. Deeply troubling."

"Do you want currant jelly or blueberry jam?"

She didn't answer.

"Butter?"

Still no answer.

Bill waited. He wasn't sure what to say. Liz took the toast from the toaster and put it on two plates; then she spoke again.

"I tried thinking about you. Didn't work."

"Sorry."

"It wasn't your fault. Evil kept intruding."

Bill buttered his toast. "It's hard to know what to do."

Liz still stood by the toaster. "Yes, it is. Our options are very limited. But we have to act."

"I agree."

"We can't simply accept the terrible harm this government is doing."

"One of the problems of democracy is that sometimes people vote wrong."

"I don't think the people voted for this."

"It's hard to know. Look at the polling numbers about Chicago. Most people liked the police rough stuff they saw on TV, or they wanted the police to be even tougher. The people who are saying that are permitted to vote."

"We can't accept immorality."

"No. Are you just going to have dry toast?"

Liz didn't answer the question. "We have to fight back."

"Is that the conclusion of your sleepless night?"

"I suppose it is." She finally sat at the table. "You're not going to tell me what to do. "

"No, of course not. Where did that remark come from?"

"I've been thinking about it."

"Good. Me, too."

"I have my own ideas. You're a strong guy, but I'm strong, too."

"I know you are." He met her eyes. "And I don't mess around with people who rowed crew." He looked away. "Let's be careful about this. I don't want SDS to break us apart."

Liz said, "Why should that happen?"

"We're still getting to know each other. There could be a misunderstanding."

"It'll help if we listen to each other."

Bill had a mouthful of toast, but managed to say, "Yes."

Liz said, "Listen with our hearts."

Bill bowed his head. "I'm all for that, but I don't think it means that we don't need to be rational."

Liz pressed him. "Does 'rational' mean heartless or self-serving?"

"Of course not."

"I hope not"

Liz started to eat her toast. Bill retreated. He was thinking about how best to maintain his cover but not endorse violence and not lose her. A neat trick.

Liz frowned. Then she cried.

Bill put his arms around her and she nestled her head on his shoulder. He said, "We'll get through this."

She replied, "That's not the point."

He hugged her. "Yes, it is. Ultimately, it's the best we usually do."

Christmas, 1968, the apartment

They were decorating a small balsam, about three feet tall, set up in the living room by the front windows on a stand that came from Kresge's. They put red cloth around the base of the tree and there was a strand of small white lights draped across the branches. As Bill hung candy canes on the tree, he ate several.

Liz said, "You're putting on weight."

"That's because I'm happy. I'm eating, and you're making me happy. When I was angry and depressed, then I was in fighting trim, lean. I had that lean and hungry look."

"Such men are dangerous."

"Ah, Bryn Mawr. You know the line."

"Actually, it comes from listening to my father."

Bill put another candy cane on the tree and then looked at Liz. "I'm trying to figure you out. You want a revolution, you want to turn things upside down and shake them. Angry people do that sort of thing, but you don't seem angry. You're kind, loving."

She didn't answer. Bill concluded that his remark was unwelcome, but Liz simply hummed "O Come All Ye Faithful".

He said, "Should I lose some weight? That'll make me cranky."

"I don't want you cranky."

"I should go to the gym more, maybe do some boxing."

"No, don't box. You'll get a black eye and then people will think I'm beating you up."

"It's easy to be a slug in this cold weather."

"Better a slug than a slugger."

"There's a slogan for a pacifist T-shirt."

February 13, 1969, Ann Arbor, encrypted telex

To: Charles Maranville, Director, Domestic Operations

From: Burke

Mostly old news. It turns out that the new strain of radicals has a short growing season. In the winter, they go dormant. In any event, it is quiet here. Ann Arbor is cold in February, so the students stay inside and talk. There is, as always, a great deal of talk in the SDS.

The main topic of conversation continues to be the split between the Progressive Labor faction, called PL, and the activists (for want of a better label). Here at U of M, that latter group calls themselves "the Jesse James gang," to make the point that they are outlaws, I suppose. The PL is ideological, now very fond of Chairman Mao. There is endless discussion of doctrinal distinctions between Russian and Chinese communism. The clear preference here is for Chinese. The Third World is popular. The Jesse James gang, however, is not interested in ideology—doesn't know much about it and cares less. They want action. As a result, there are now, in effect, two SDS chapters at U of M and they compete for student support. The Jesse James gang is aligned with and supported by the SDS national office in Chicago.

The split weakens SDS overall. They can't agree on a strategy or plan of action, so not much happens. When there is an initiative, it isn't successful. For example, the attempt in November to take over the U of M administration building, including the president's office, was abortive—student turnout

117

was small, and we were chased out of the building after only five hours. There were no heroics.

I've chosen to ally myself with the Jesse James gang because it is clearly the more dangerous element, the one that needs watching.

Reports from other campuses suggest a similar situation. The police violence in Chicago aided SDS recruitment, but that was a short-term effect. When the student recruits went to SDS meetings and heard nothing but ideological gibberish and bickering about what to do next, they were turned off. Since membership is a flexible concept, there is no clear measure, but I think student support is now down. My overall assessment is that SDS is less of a threat to the nation today than it was six months ago. But that could change. The non-ideological element is unmoored and unpredictable.

The change may come with warm weather. These folks are fair weather revolutionaries. Perhaps they are students of history and know about Washington's soldiers at Valley Forge, with their feet wrapped in rags, or perhaps they have in mind Napoleon's troops freezing in Russia's snow and ice, and don't want their fate.

I'm finding that intelligence work has a lot of downtime. There's a great deal of sitting around listening to people say much about very little. But I'm keeping at it.

—Message terminates—

Reply:
To: Burke

From: Maranville

Yes, intelligence work requires patience. You have to cultivate the art of listening, and being in the right place at the right time inevitably requires hanging around.

Don't push for information. Don't cross-examine. Don't try to force it. Surveillance seldom works. You need to be there in the ordinary course of things. And, for God's sake, don't provoke violence or criminal acts. We don't want to hand them an entrapment defense.

Stay in touch.

—Message terminates—

March 6, 1969, Ann Arbor

At the kitchen table, Bill tried to type one of his concocted ghost-writing projects. It was difficult to work up enthusiasm for that, and some of the projects were pretty lame. Then Liz arrived. It was midnight and she had been working at the bar. She was full of the latest news.

"Willy, do you remember a guy we met in East Lansing named Oscar Cameron? We called him Ozzie. He was one of the teachers at the panel on bombing techniques. We had dinner with him and Hal."

"Yeah, I guess maybe so." Bill pushed his chair back.

"You remember. Skinny kid from Colorado. Went to Colorado State in Fort Collins, and Hal was asking him a lot of questions about dynamite."

"Okay, if you say so."

"Well, it turns out that Ozzie was serious about bombing. He's now been convicted of dynamiting high voltage transmission towers in Colorado. The lines were supplying power to a company that manufactures the nose cones for Sidewinder missiles. The bombs shut down the plant, temporarily."

"I thought you told me that the bombing panel in East Lansing was just for show."

"Yeah, well I guess not entirely."

"So Cameron is locked up now?"

"No, he got away."

"But you said he got convicted."

"He wasn't there for the trial."

"Can they do that?"

"I guess so."

"Did he go to Canada or somewhere?"

"Nobody knows. Or nobody is talking. He's disappeared. Gone underground."

"It's usually dark and cold underground."

Liz took her jacket off and poured a glass of milk. "When you put this together with the bombing of the ROTC building at Washington University in St. Louis, it begins to look like a new phase of the struggle."

"The guy who did the St. Louis one is now in jail."

Liz walked to a window and looked out. "Have you ever been to the Washington U. campus?" She was far away.

"No. I've never been to St. Louis."

"I visited the campus when I went to the Veiled Prophet hoopla. I considered going to Washington U. for college. It has

a pretty campus on the west edge of the city, right next to Forest Park, which has the art museum, the zoo, and an outdoor
theater. The campus has pink granite buildings in a style called
Tudor Gothic, except that they didn't start building it until about
1900, for the St. Louis World's Fair. I'll bet you know the movie.
You always do. Judy Garland riding the streetcar. 'Meet me in St.
Louie, Louie.' It's a shame that we have to blow it up."

"Yeah."

June 18-22, 1969, Chicago

The Coliseum was a dingy grey building on South Wabash Street,
a dingy grey part of town. The day was also grey and it was cool
for June. A vacant school across the street provided convenient
windows for police photographers who took pictures with tele-
photo lenses of the arriving SDS delegates, newspaper and TV
journalists, and undercover cops. The street was crowded, but no
uniformed police were visible. The Chamber of Commerce had
made it clear to the mayor that the City's hotels and restaurants
couldn't afford more bad publicity. Conventions would go else-
where. Word came down from the mayor's office that there was
not to be another confrontation.

The SDS was not letting reporters into the Coliseum, but
some young ones got in by claiming to be students and paying
the five dollar registration fee. The security personnel screening
the registrants had a simple test: "Where do you go to school?"
Answer: "Kansas State." "Name a professor in the English department." Answer: "Professor James." "Okay." Professor James

usually worked. The security personnel were students with green armbands. The green armband was their only obvious qualification. One reporter made the mistake of saying "University of Wisconsin" and the screener was a student there. When she asked for the name of a professor in the English department, the reporter said that he was a sociology major and didn't remember the English professors. "Okay, then name one of the bars near the campus." Answer: "The Var Bar." Response: "My favorite place." The reporter had visited Madison.

Liz and Bill arrived on time, but the meeting started five hours late. The interior of the building was also grey. It was a complex of halls, one big auditorium and a number of smaller rooms that were useful for caucuses and rump meetings. It rented for $440 a day, without chairs. Eighteen hundred temporary chairs had been brought in. Unfortunately, it was possible to throw them.

The first vote of any consequence concerned journalists. The SDS national office presented a motion proposing that reporters be permitted to enter the hall if they paid a $25 fee. The fee would help defray the expenses of the convention. The motion specified that recording equipment would not be allowed, however, and that the *New York Times* would not be eligible for entry because one of its reporters had testified about SDS before the House Internal Security Committee. A delegate from the PL faction took the microphone. He wanted all journalists banned from the meeting.

"We shouldn't let any reporters in. The capitalist press is not going to print the truth. They'll distort what happens. They always distort. We have our own press."

When the issue came to a vote, the national office lost by

a margin of 60% to 40%, and the leadership saw that it was in trouble.

Liz turned to Bill. "PL has packed the hall. They did a better job of turning out the troops."

Bill said, "Yeah, the national office is going to continue losing. We don't have the votes. What do we do now?"

Liz was calm. "You and I will just keep quiet, mostly, and then we vote right when the time comes. Hannah and Mike and Mark will figure out something, I hope. We'll wait and see, unless you have a better idea."

"Well, we need an issue we can win on."

Liz thought a minute, then said, "You're right. How about women's lib? The leadership of PL has been pretty much all male for years. They've done nothing for women. We have Hannah, and she's prominent, visible."

Bill agreed. "Yes. She's a real leader."

"I'll talk to her."

But PL had also discovered women's lib. The result was that both factions issued strong statements supporting women's rights. There was little space between the two sides on the issue, and women had no real reason to prefer one on that ground.

Liz and Bill waited for something to happen while votes were taken on a number of minor issues to test the ability of the two factions to mobilize their delegates and hold them in line. The national office appeared to be losing.

Friday afternoon, June 20, Hannah told Liz, "The Black Panthers think the formal Marxist ideology of PL is a waste of time, and the Panthers have confronted police and not backed down. The convention will listen to the Panthers. I think I can get Chaka Walls, an Illinois Panther, to address the convention and attack PL. "

Later that afternoon, Walls made an impressive entrance. He wore dark wraparound glasses and was surrounded by Panther bodyguards. He had presence, but his speech did not go as well as his entrance. Among other things, he said, "We believe in pussy power." There were murmurs from the floor, then shouts. The PL faction chanted: "Fight Male Chauvinism." The Coliseum was a barn, and it had a good echo. The chant reverberated. The building was used for roller-derbies. It was perfect for that.

Coarse language was just fine—Mark Rudd specialized in it; it was transgressive, and that was the SDS style—but sexist imagery was out of bounds. Walls alienated a clear majority of the delegates. The national office was stunned. Hannah was on good terms with the Panthers, but she couldn't dictate their speech and she hadn't expected what she got.

Bill turned to Liz again. "Well, that sure didn't work. Jesus! What do we do now?"

"Regroup, I suppose. I don't know what Hannah and Mike will come up with."

By that evening, they devised a do-over, but it turned into a replay. They recruited another Panther leader, Jewell Cook, to speak at seven p.m. The plan, probably, was that he would be conciliatory, perhaps apologetic. He was not.

He began his speech with an all-out denunciation of PL. That was not what the national office had intended, but it was acceptable. Then he said, "I'm with my brother (Walls) in this. I'm for pussy power myself. You sisters have a strategic position in the revolution. The position for you sisters is prone." The shouts began again. The PL resumed "Fight Male Chauvism," even louder. The national office constituency, including Liz and Bill, then tried the Panther slogan, "Power to the People." The PL switched to "Power to the Workers." Cook didn't finish his speech.

SDS chapters based primarily in the Midwest—Michigan, Ohio, and Chicago, with some participants from New York and some from the San Francisco Bay area—supported the national office. That loosely organized group called itself "Weatherman." But there was disagreement among its leaders about tactics, forceful disagreement. They huddled at the back of the stage. Mark Rudd proposed a recess of the Convention, with it scheduled to resume in an hour. Hannah was having none of that. She was obviously furious, and she argued heatedly with Rudd and Mike Klonsky, the elected leader of SDS (known as the National Secretary). Klonsky tried to restrain her, but Meyer broke away.

She took the microphone. She said that her principles did not permit her to remain in an organization with people "who deny the right of self-determination to the oppressed." She then invited anyone who shared her view to join her in another room in the building. She walked off the stage and down a corridor on the left. After an awkward pause, Rudd and then Klonsky followed her. The Michigan, Chicago, and Ohio delegates, including Liz and Bill, walked out next. The PL constituency chanted, "Sit Down!" then "Stay and Fight." Slowly, hesitantly at first, about a third of the delegates followed Meyer to a smaller hall off the main floor. Those who had walked out talked for the next three hours, expressing the full range of possible views and some not so possible. At midnight they stopped talking and adjourned for the night.

Saturday was the final day of the convention. Hannah Meyer once again took the microphone. She made a twenty-minute speech, reciting the sins and errors of PL, at the end of which she delivered the punch line. "The Progressive Labor Party is objectively racist, anti-communist, and reactionary. Progressive Labor Party members, and all others who do not accept our principles, are no longer members of SDS." She then left the stage and once again walked out. The PL began to shout, "Shame! Shame!" But there was none. The Meyer faction still had the keys to the national office.

Liz and Bill returned to Ann Arbor on Sunday, upset by the unresolved conflict and very tired.

Monday, June 23, 1969, Ann Arbor

For his report to Rabbit, Bill used a telephone booth at the Cozy Corner Bar, two miles from the campus. The guys at the bar were watching a game between the Tigers and the Yankees, broadcast from Tiger Stadium. The Tigers were winning and the customers weren't interested in the phone call.

"It was quite a show in Chicago. I'm not entirely sure what the fallout will be. You've probably already seen some of the news accounts."

"Write it up and file a report as usual, but first give me your summary."

"Well, at one level, it was hilarious, all carried out with a straight face—no, even funnier than that. It was carried out with frowns and snarls and grimaces. It was a cross between Buster Keaton and Harold Lloyd, or maybe Charlie Chaplin in *The Great Dictator*. Crazy stuff."

"Not many of my agents give me popular culture references. I've got to be careful about hiring film majors."

"I wasn't a film major, just a member of the film club. But I didn't tell Liz or any of the hots about the cultural references, and I didn't laugh."

"No, that would have been unprofessional."

"Yeah. Never, never laugh at their very serious meetings." Bill laughed. "Hannah Meyer was either out of control or doing a good acting job. It may well have been the latter."

Rabbit wanted substance. "Now that we've dealt with the entertainment value, tell me what happened, as you evaluate it."

"The Chicago group, led by Meyer, simply seized power. Although they were clearly in the minority at the convention, they just declared that they were the SDS. They did what Senator Aiken said we should do in Vietnam, they declared victory and went home. De facto, they now have the power. They have control of the organization's office on West Madison Street, so they have the records, the mailing lists and addresses, the bank accounts (such as they are), and the printing press. But they've probably lost half the members, maybe more. The ruling clique includes Meyer, Klonsky, Rudd, Jacobs, Jones, and Bissell. It also includes Jim Mellor, an interesting case. Mellor proposed that the expulsion of PL be put to a vote of the convention. He argued that it should be democratic. If it had been, the national office would have lost. So Meyer, Klonsky, et al., put the kibosh on that. There are those who suspect that Mellor is a PL operative, or maybe even FBI. I think he may be a Chinese agent. He has PL in his history."

"That's interesting. I don't have anything for you on that."

"The turning point came on Friday when national's invited speaker, a Black Panther, said that he believed in 'pussy power.' Then another Panther speaker said that the place for women in the movement was 'prone.' The place went wild. The SDS is an organization of college kids, who are all for sex, but the Panthers were not on the same wavelength as those college kids."

"What happens now?"

"Well, the Weatherman faction is in control."

"What does Weatherman mean?"

"Weatherman is what the Chicago leadership group, Meyer et al., call themselves now. The name comes from a Bob Dylan song. The idea is that radicals need to know which way the wind is blowing, unlike the PL ideology. The Weathermen are clearly the more dangerous, more violent players. They say, and I believe them, that there will now be more dynamite, more bombings."

"What can we do to stop them?"

"The main thing we need is information. We need to know where and when they plan to strike. To get that, we have to have assets on the inside. I could use some help. I don't know what the FBI is doing."

"I don't either, and they aren't going to tell me. They'll just tell us to stay out of it."

"Can they handle it?"

"No, they're incompetent."

Bill didn't argue the point. "We could try to close off sources of dynamite, but that'll be difficult. I suppose we could try to track the movement of explosives, but they come from many different directions, mostly from construction projects, from what I hear. Hard to stop that."

Rabbit asked a standard question. "Where does their money come from?"

"I don't really think they spend much money. They sleep on floors and eat dry breakfast cereal. I think they steal the dynamite. Many of them receive small amounts of money from their parents, but we can't tell mom and dad not to send a few bucks to Little Susie."

"Maybe mom and dad would like to know what the kid is doing."

"That's okay with me, so long as we can do it without disclosing our assets."

"Yes. That's the trick. Please write it up."

"Will do."

Five

Bill stewed. The dynamite had raised the stakes. The damn stuff was too easy to get — the cops would never be able to cut off the supply, and bombs were easy to make. As much as he hated to do it, Bill thought he needed to put more pressure on Liz. Maybe he could get more information from her. Or maybe, even better for her, he could persuade her to back away from the Weathermen.

Bill went into the living room, where Liz was reading. "Look, I'm sure that Weatherman can get its hands on explosives and guns, and probably has already, but do you really know what we're up against, what we're going to have to fight? The police, the FBI, the National Guard, the Army. They have a hell of a lot more firepower than we do and a lot more troops. We can't beat them. Not even close. The Vietnamese can defeat our army, but they're fighting on their own turf, defending their own country. Here, the army and the cops might just regard this as their country, especially since they appear to own it."

Liz turned to face Bill. "We don't have to fight head-on. We just need to undermine the regime enough to weaken its author-

130

ity. When the people see that resistance is possible and that a revolution is underway, is happening, they'll rise up and join us. We already chased Johnson out of office. We can do the same to Nixon. We only need to show that the country is ungovernable. To govern means to command allegiance. When the government can no longer do that, then the game's over."

"This isn't a game, Liz. Before any of that happens, people will be killed, probably lots of them."

"People are being killed in Vietnam right now, lots of them. Do the deaths of Vietnamese not count?"

"Why is violence necessary? Why can't we just make an appeal to decency, to morality—just persuade people that the war is wrong, immoral? The war's already unpopular."

"The trouble is that this war is too easy for Americans. It's on the other side of the world. Americans can ignore it. And they do. LBJ told us that we can have both guns and butter. That we can afford it. It's painless. We need to make the war painful here, not just in Vietnam. We need to bring the war home so that Americans have to make a choice."

"I confess that when it's closer to home, when it's my brothers and sisters, my parents that we're talking about, it puts a different face on it. Have you ever killed anyone, Liz?"

"No, of course not."

"Have you ever killed an animal?"

"No. Have you?"

"I shot a rabbit once, with a small-gauge shotgun. I felt bad about it. It isn't pretty."

"It's a question of fundamental morality, Willy. At some point … at *some* point, you have to be willing to set aside self-interest and do the right thing even if it risks your life or the lives of people you love. Otherwise, you let evil win, and everyone gets harmed."

"That all sounds pretty neat, pretty cut and dried, but I think the reality is a lot messier."

"At some point, you have to cut through all the crap, all the obfuscation. There are real principles involved. At some point."

"Do you want to die, Liz?"

"No, of course I don't want to die. But I do want a better world, a world where children won't be burned alive by napalm just to satisfy the greed of capitalists."

Bill dug into the pockets of his jeans. He seemed to be searching for something, but he didn't produce anything. "And you think 'the people' will rise up and support the revolution. Who are those people? Look around you. Most of our citizens aren't like the comfortable boys and girls who went to the Upperville School or Bryn Mawr or Colgate and who spend their time reading Regis Debray. Most people go to work every day, many of them to jobs they don't like, and they do it to put food on the table and a roof over their heads. Their needs are relatively simple. They don't spend their time grappling with big theoretical questions, and they don't take big risks. They can't afford to. They aren't going to rise up so long as they're fed. Not the white ones anyhow. Maybe the black people might rise up, they have more reason to, but they aren't going to be led by you or me. And they would be overwhelmed in an all-out race war."

"So, what's your solution? What should we do?"

"We need to keep trying to persuade people to vote right. We need to persuade them that the Vietnam War is wrong and racism is wrong and wage slavery is wrong, and that they shouldn't elect politicians who support those things."

"That hasn't worked, Willy. It's been tried. It's been tried over and over again. It doesn't work. That sort of thinking got us where we are today. The power structure has too much control. They control the news media. They control the elections. We have to take it away from them. By force, if necessary."

Bill pressed harder. "We saw what the Chicago police were willing to do. Even when the news media condemned it, the public supported the police, overwhelmingly. Next time they'll shoot to kill. What you're messing with is extremely dangerous."

"I'm not messing with anything. I'm working for an important cause — an imperative — and I've thought about how to do it. Messing with! You should have more respect for me than that, for Christ's sake."

"I do respect you, Liz. I also love you, as I've said before. It's because I respect and love you so much that I care deeply about what happens to you. I don't want you to be hurt, irreparably hurt. What you're doing can change your life."

"Of course it can change my life — for the better, I hope. But I recognize that there'll be pain in the process. That's exactly the problem with you. You lack commitment. You want it to be painless. You aren't willing to pay the price. I am. It's my choice. I'm doing what I think is right. I wish you had the courage to do the same."

"You should think hard about why you're doing this. The Weathermen are hell-bent on serious violence, whether it makes any sense or not." Liz frowned at Bill and Bill frowned back. He tried another tack. "I don't get it. Are you rebelling against something? Was your father extremely strict? Was your mother just a conventional housewife, so you're determined to be a strong woman?"

"What gives you the right to ask that?"

"My love for you."

Liz pushed hair out of her eyes. "Am I supposed to take those questions seriously?"

"Why not give it a try?"

She paused. "My father. He's reasonable; he's devoted to being reasonable. He was always busy at the bank and in the legislature, so he really wasn't around much, which was reasonable. My mother. No, she wasn't an ordinary housewife. We had a cook and a nanny, and for a while there was also a housemaid, what we called a 'serving girl.' A cleaning lady came in once a week. Together, they were 'the help.' Mom knows how to sew, but she doesn't have much use for the skill. She was never much of a cook, but she enjoyed making jams and angel food cakes. To make a cake, she would sit in the kitchen and say, 'Mary, bring me a whisk.' Mary was the serving girl. Maybe that's something that should be rebelled against."

"So you'll be much happier in the classless society."

"I may or may not be happier, as you put it, but the people who don't have enough to eat will be healthier and happier." Liz put her coat on and picked up her backpack.

Bill persisted. "Bombs are a terrible weapon. It's very hard to control who gets hurt. The bomber walks away and then innocent people get blown up or hit by shrapnel. But at least bombs might possibly bring change. They cause terror, and terror changes people's actions. Bombs might make a government willing to negotiate. But what good is vandalism? What good is breaking windows? What good is setting fires in trash cans? All that does is piss people off. It doesn't persuade them. It isn't working, Liz. The people aren't rising up. American workers don't want a revolution. They want cars and a house with a TV set. The revolution isn't happening. It's failed. Don't throw your life away. You can't force your sort of government on people who don't want it."

Liz opened the door and started to leave. But then she changed her mind, went back in, took off her hat and coat, and sat down. She said, "The whites in the suburbs have to feel the pain. We won't get change until the whites with money feel it."

Bill leaned back and looked at the ceiling. "My background is different from yours. I grew up with a different set of expectations. The small furniture store that my father and his two brothers owned barely supported the three families, and it sure wasn't going to support another generation. For you, and for most of the Weathermen, it was different. You and Bill Bissell, Mark Rudd, Cathy Wilkerson, Kathy Boudin, and so on, grew up with plenty of money. You never had to think about what you were going to do for a living. Oh, you probably had dreams, but you never had to really worry about it. You knew you would be taken care of. Maybe you didn't have the talent to be a concert pianist, but you could own a good piano. That gave you a kind of freedom, the freedom to make choices. Unfortunately, it seems to me, it also freed you from responsibility. You didn't have to answer to anyone. You were invincible. Put most harshly, that's a form of arrogance. You are quieter, more subtle, nicer, than Bissell or Rudd, but the underlying problem is similar. It's the problem of privilege—a terrible curse. You don't have to consider the possibility that you might be wrong, that you might be doing the wrong thing."

Liz stood up and crossed the room. "Have you finished? Who is the arrogant bastard here? You're the one lecturing me. What have I done to deserve it? I try to do what will be best for society, even though there'll be personal sacrifice. Why do you get to make the choices? Is that because you're male? And here you are, simply floating through life. I don't see you writing much, or publishing under your own name, taking responsibility. If you're trying to persuade me of something, you're doing a damn poor job of it."

"I'm sorry. I'm just trying to keep you from getting hurt, maybe seriously hurt. We're from different social classes, and we're talking past each other. There's a barrier that we can't get over and I find that sad. I think you're making some very bad choices."

"Then we're even." Liz put her coat and hat back on, ready to leave. "I don't think the difference between us has much, or maybe anything, to do with social class. I think it's a question of moral ambition. How many of the wrongs that you see will you dare to change? Will you try to make society better? I don't want to just make a living. I want to have my life count for something."

Bill remained seated. "How much self-confidence does it take to believe that you can re-make society? To believe that you can overcome the social, economic, and cultural forces that have put us where we are today? To reverse the course of history?"

September 1969, Ann Arbor

Bill and Liz were at the bar. It was raining, and there were no customers. Business had fallen off since the split in SDS after the walkout at the Chicago Coliseum, but the leaders of Weatherman were planning a multi-day rally in Chicago that they were calling the National Action. No date or specific program had been announced, but people were being urged to make this a show of force.

Bill said, "I don't think I can go with you."

"Why not?"

"In Chicago, that cop will be looking for me."

"The one with a broken nose?"

"That's the one."

" …and the dislocated shoulder?"

"That too."

"We could disguise you."

"Okay. I want to be Superman, or maybe Zorro."

"How about a cop?"

"I think it's a crime to wear a military uniform or a law enforcement uniform if you're not entitled to it."

"You won't need a uniform. First, shave off your beard. That'll help a lot. Then get a short haircut and put on a suit and tie. A sport coat and khakis would work. But you'll need a white shirt. The cop would never recognize you."

"I'll look like an assistant professor."

"You'll look like a detective. There'll be lots of them there. You'll blend in. They won't shoot someone dressed like that."

"And will you wear a little black dress and a strand of pearls?"

"Damn it, Willy, this is serious! You don't have the right attitude. Nixon is bombing Cambodia. That's why we're going to Chicago. The bombing in Cambodia has to stop. If it doesn't, there'll be bombs here."

September 1969, Another meeting with BJ

Bill sat at the guest chair in BJ's cubicle. "The Weathermen are turning up the heat now. Do you agree with their strategy, raising the stakes? Is this going to improve our chances?"

BJ put on the glasses he wore when he wasn't reading. "I don't think they know what they're doing. They're too enthusiastic about the fight. There's no point in fighting just for the sake of fighting, or just to show that they're capable of doing it."

"They think black people will rise up and join them."

"Good luck with that. The blacks won't follow whitey."

"Do you think the movement is going to succeed?"

BJ turned the question to Bill. "Do you have doubts?"

"No, not really," Bill answered hesitantly.

"Well you should."

"What do you mean?"

"Okay, here we go. Whether the movement is going to succeed, or whether I think it is? Well, forgive me for sounding like a philosopher, but we need to define your terms."

Bill asked, "Which terms?"

"First, what do you mean by 'the movement'?"

"I mean us, SDS, the revolution."

"But you know as well as I that many of the people in SDS

don't agree on goals. They don't all want the same kind of society. But let's leave to one side the conflicts within SDS—maybe those might be resolved—probably not. In any case, I surely don't have the same goals as the Yippies, as Abbie Hoffman and Jerry Rubin. And Dr. King's Southern Christian Leadership Conference doesn't agree with the Yippies, or the Black Panthers, or Stokely Carmichael, or Rap Brown, or Angela Davis. And then, of course, there's the Communist Party and Progressive Labor. There are a lot of different revolutions to choose from."

"But they all want a different sort of society," Bill retorted. "And most of them, at least, want an end to the Vietnam War."

"Yes, but the various factions would surely not accept each other's terms for ending the war. If they defeated Richard Nixon, they would then fight battles with each other. But let's move on to the next problematic term: What do you mean by 'succeed'?"

"Well, first of all, I mean an end to the war."

BJ asked, "Would you accept any or all outcomes in order to achieve that? Would you accept terms in which we dominate Vietnam? Or they dominate us? 'Peace now' is just a slogan. It isn't a treaty or an accord. Maybe we just withdraw, walk away. But that doesn't solve North Vietnam's problems with the South and vice versa, or the Buddhists' problems with the Catholics, and it also doesn't solve Vietnam's problems with its neighbors. They might slaughter each other. Should we care about any of that?"

"Maybe it isn't our responsibility."

"Our fellow man? Well, then let's also suppose the Vietnam problem is solved: We just walk away and let them collapse or kill each other. So, closer to home, do you care about racial justice, about lousy or non-existent education, poverty, housing, starvation, child welfare, women's rights, nuclear weapons, the death penalty? I'm sure you do. Some more than others, perhaps. People who call themselves part of the movement certainly disagree on those things. Success for one constituency would not be success for another."

"Does that mean we'll inevitably fail? Or just that we won't get everything?"

"Good question, Willy. I'm not sure. If success means overcoming all of the interest groups arrayed against us, do I think we'll achieve that? No, I do not. There are too many of them, and they're too powerful. They have too many guns, too many newspapers, too many TV stations, too much money. There would be blood spilled. Too much blood. The poor would suffer most, as always. But I think the question of success might be redefined as whether we will get enough justice, enough additional justice, to be worth the sacrifice, the risk, the price. I do think that if the revolutionary movement could disrupt society enough to make people uncomfortable and dissatisfied, then we might, *might* upset the established order. So, then, so defined, what are the odds of our success? To be honest, I think they're less than fifty-fifty. Does that mean we shouldn't try? No, it doesn't. If we could have, say, only a twenty-five percent chance of securing significant justice, we should certainly go for it. It would be worth the risk. Then we should sacrifice ourselves, if necessary."

"Are you going to make a speech saying we have only a twenty-five percent chance of success?"

"I don't make speeches." BJ smiled. "I talk, but I don't do speeches."

"Perhaps you should. It might open some eyes." Bill scratched his head. "Would you be willing to talk to Liz? She seems to be persuaded by the Weatherman line."

"Sure, I'd talk if she wants to talk. But I don't know that I would change her mind."

Bill leaned forward. "I've tried to persuade her. Every time I try to say that violence is the wrong way to go, we end up arguing, and the argument then drives her farther into the Weatherman camp. In answering me, opposing me—and asserting her independence, I suppose—it turns into a contest that she wants to win, and she becomes more confident that we should use violence and bombings. I seem to drive her away from me and toward Hannah and Hal. I think I'm just hardening her."

"Well, sure," said BJ. "That's a common process of reaction. Didn't you have a parent you rebelled against? If you can see it happening, why do you persist? Why don't you try being more uncertain, or more sympathetic, or just supportive without pushing?"

"I'm not by nature very subtle. I'm afraid she's going to get hurt. But Liz is clearly sincere, clearly devoted to our cause, and she's trying to figure things out, trying to get it right."

"I think most of us are trying to get it right." BJ picked up a book and took off his glasses, preparing to get back to work. "The reasons why people do things are often obscure. In fact, talking about decisions in terms of reasons makes it sound like an intellectual process, but only a minority of decisions are made that way. Some are instinctual, almost automatic, some are impulsive, some are emotional. But calling it impulse, instinct, or emotion suggests motivations that are ill-considered, if considered at all, which makes those decisions sound second-rate. They are only irrational in the sense that ratiocination was not what determined the result. They are not *ipso facto* wrong or counter-productive. Why should ratiocination be preferred? We know that reasoning is highly imperfect. It doesn't always lead to the right answer, certainly. The mind is one thing, the soul is something else. Is the product of the mind necessarily better than that of the soul? The mind may tell you not to proceed, but the soul may dictate that you must. I think I would often prefer the decision that comes from the soul — or the heart."

October 8-11, 1969, Chicago

The Weathermen, including both Bill and Liz, assembled at the south end of Lincoln Park not far from the Cardinal's residence, near the spot where Bill broke the policeman's nose the year before. The City expected the protesters to refuse to leave the park at the eleven p.m. curfew, as many had the year before. Police in riot gear surrounded the park. There was no National Guard this time, but disobedience would not be tolerated. The Chicago Police Department would handle it, with enthusiasm. They had a score to settle.

There was, or had been, a monument in Chicago honoring seven police officers who were killed at Haymarket Square in a confrontation with anarchists in 1886. The businessmen who had been the targets of the anarchists responded by erecting a statue dedicated to the memory of the fallen officers. It was a ten foot tall bronze policeman, standing on a twelve foot tall marble pedestal, but two nights before the gathering in Lincoln Park, in the middle of the night, a small band of Weathermen, not including either Bill or Liz, visited the statue. They placed dynamite, attached a fuse, retired a safe distance, and detonated the bomb. Perhaps significantly, the charge was placed between the policeman's legs. The detonation was extensive. Pieces of the statue were blown onto the Kennedy Expressway. Scores of windows in neighboring buildings were broken. The perpetrators were not caught.

Bill had heard the news and visited the site. He said to Liz, "Have you seen it? Our boys did a messy job. When the IRA brought down Nelson's Pillar in Dublin two or three years ago, they did it with surgical precision. But, then, the IRA men had had the benefit of training in the British army. They toppled half of the whole granite column, and it was big enough to have a spiral staircase inside and an observation platform at the top, right in the center of Dublin. I went up it once."

"You were in Dublin?"

"Oh yes, I went to visit the ancestral home of the Felds."

Liz laughed.

Bill was pleased with himself. "I called it the Guinness Tour."

The president of a police union said that the destruction of the Haymarket statue was a message: "kill or be killed." The rhetoric on both sides was apocalyptic, but the Weathermen hadn't mobilized enough troops for the apocalypse. In recent months, Weatherman leaders had called for, had predicted, a turnout of thousands for the National Action. There had been at least three thousand protesters in Grant Park during the Democratic convention the year before. But so far only two hundred or so potential combatants had arrived. The riot police persuaded some to turn back, but there weren't many willing fighters to begin with.

The Weathermen had gas masks, were armed with lengths of pipe and chains, and many wore white motorcycle helmets, but there were simply not enough of them. The leaders waited. Hannah Meyer, Bill Bissell, and Jeff Jones were a hundred yards inside the park, gathered around a large bonfire that had been built with wood from the park's benches, broken up for the purpose. A few more protesters arrived, maybe as many as a hundred more, providing a total of perhaps three hundred, but the police had canceled days off and had mobilized two thousand uniformed officers. There were also a large number of plainclothesmen in the park. Bill was trying to be one of the plainclothesmen, but that was dangerous because many of the City's detectives knew each other. They did not, however, know the FBI agents brought in from around the country, and this was to Bill's advantage.

When there were no more park benches to use for fuel, Weathermen broke fence railings and added them to the fading bonfire. Bill didn't participate. He liked the wooden fence, but he had to restrain himself. He couldn't intervene. There would be more serious harm to be prevented later. Bill wondered how long Weatherman's leaders could stall. At the curfew, police would move into the Park. The Weathermen did not intend to wait for them.

Through a bullhorn, Hannah told the crowd that this was the second anniversary of Che Guevara's death and that their mission was to advance the revolution for Che. Then Jeff Jones took the bullhorn and boomed, "I am Marion Delgado," and the Weathermen began to move. Marion Delgado was the signal. It was the name of a five-year old boy who had derailed a train with a concrete block. When the signal came, Liz was not where Bill could see her. He had been warming himself at the bonfire and, after looking at the flames, his eyes were not accustomed to the darkness. Liz disappeared in the surge of Weathermen. She was wearing a white helmet, a sweatshirt and sweatpants, but so were many of the others. This didn't help single her out. And she didn't have a weapon.

Bill knew that he would have to be careful. He was dressed as a plainclothes cop, but he wasn't armed, didn't have a helmet, and being arrested would certainly blow his cover because the Agency would have to intervene to get the charges dropped. He would need to stay out of the crowd. He couldn't be moving with the leaders, which he thought was probably where Liz could be found. He was right.

Most of the Weathermen had already charged out of the park into the Gold Coast neighborhood. The police had not expected them to move so soon and were taken by surprise. The Weathermen broke through the police line and then divided into three main groups. One headed toward the Drake Hotel overlooking Lake Michigan and the beach along Lake Shore Drive. Judge Julius Hoffman, who was presiding over the federal trial of the leaders of the demonstrations the year before, was living at the Drake. A second group went toward Astor Street, the elegant heart of the Gold Coast with Mon Petit restaurant, the Park Dearborn Hotel, and Maxim's. A third went west from the park toward the Old Town and Lincoln Park residential neighborhoods. All three forces were pursued by police.

Liz was near the front of the large group advancing toward the Drake. She was running. They were all running. Hal was beside her. As they neared the Drake, they saw a barrier across the intersection. Blue lights on top of the police cars were revolving and making patterns on the glass curtain walls of the high-rise apartment buildings. The City may have anticipated an assault on the hotel, perhaps because of Judge Hoffman's presence there or perhaps because the hotel was famous and a well-known symbol of privilege. Police blocked the intersection with an armed force standing two deep. Liz thought it would be crazy to charge into them. She said as much to Hal, who didn't answer.

Liz could feel her heart pounding. She was out of breath—she wasn't used to running this far or this fast. But she felt good! It was exhilarating to be doing instead of just talking. She felt that she was finally making a real contribution to the cause, putting herself on the line, taking some risk. Was it fun? Well, yes, she supposed that it was; it was certainly satisfying.

When the Weatherman vanguard was within half a block of the police barricade, the leaders turned, detoured around the hotel via Rush Street, and then continued south along Michigan Avenue. Liz didn't know the streets. She and Hal were moving fast, but they stopped to break things. Along with other Weathermen, they shattered ten plate glass windows in a bank. A Rolls Royce found parked along the way was battered. Not a piece of its glass was left unbroken, and the coachwork would have to be rebuilt. But this slowed their attack. Police caught up with them, and the cops had the advantage of superior numbers and superior arms and armor. It was the same story in the other two groups. The Weathermen fought, but were quickly subdued.

Bill watched the action from the sidelines, closer to Lincoln Park. On Wells Street, in the Old Town area, three Weathermen surrounded a policeman who had become separated from his squad. The Weathermen had clubs, one of which may have been a truncheon taken from a cop, and they advanced on the officer, taunting him. Bill tried to stop them, but they took Bill for a detective and didn't stop. The policeman pulled out his pistol and shot one of the Weathermen. The young man fell. The other two Weathermen ran. Bill said to the cop, "You call a medic, I'll handle this." The bullet had gone through the kid's shoulder. Bill put pressure on the wound until the medics arrived and took over the treatment. By that time, the policeman had made himself scarce. He didn't want to have to make a shooting report, and he didn't want to be identified. There was blood on Bill's clothes.

It was all over before midnight. In all, at least six Weathermen were shot. None died. Sixty-eight protesters were arrested, including Liz. She was put into a squad car along with others and taken to a holding area.

Bill spent the next two days making telephone calls, contacting the Agency, locating the jail where Liz was held, and trying to raise money for her bail. He also had to get rid of his bloody clothes. They would attract unwanted attention. There was a clean sweatshirt and a pair of jeans in his rucksack. He had paid for the detective costume with his own money, but those clothes went into a dumpster. The Agency might reimburse him, maybe. But his cop disguise was gone. He would have to take his chances.

When he wasn't looking for Liz and trying to free her, Bill spent Thursday and Friday in the Sunday school rooms of a Methodist church. He wasn't sure whether the preacher and the sexton knew the nature of the demonstrations that their guests had planned, but they were hospitable.

The National Action, which the Weathermen later called the Days of Rage, was to be spread over four days. The assault on the

Gold Coast, the first event, took place on a Wednesday night. For Thursday's action, women in Weatherman had planned to picket a draft board office in downtown Chicago, but when the time came many of the women were in the Cook County jail with Liz. About fifty of those still free arrived at the draft board, and were met by a large force of police waiting for them. The police had an informant who told them where to be and when. Almost all of the women were immediately arrested. Liz got the news from those who joined her at the jail. Uninvited "teach-ins" at area high schools had been planned for Friday, but those were cancelled. The Weathermen had enough trouble. The leaders had difficulty communicating with their dispersed troops and trying to bail them out. The bail amounts set by judges totaled more than two million dollars.

Saturday's action was a march through the Loop, the City's main business district. It began peacefully, with relatively orderly groups of Weathermen walking down the middle of the street between solid lines of police officers along the sidewalks. This continued for a few blocks. Then, at no apparent signal, the Weathermen started running. Lengths of pipe were pulled out from under their jackets. Once again, glass started breaking in cars and stores, but police moved in quickly. All intersections were closed off so that the Weathermen could not escape. They were like cattle running into a chute. The captives were beaten with police batons.

Eventually, Liz was permitted to make a telephone call. She called her father, who came to Chicago and bailed her out. He tried to persuade her to go with him to Hiscott, to return to her family. Liz thanked him, but then went back to the Weathermen.

She was committed to the revolution. If she agonized about the decision, that was not apparent. Her father did not meet Bill.

***

Bill and Liz both missed the march. She was in jail at the time, and he wasn't pressing his luck. Their drive back to Ann Arbor was devoted to issues discussed often before. Bill drove. Getting out of the city was slow.

Liz said, "What the hell is up with the Chicago police?"

Bill was cautious at first. "Weatherman was doing serious property damage. The City hires police to stop that. That's part of it. Another part is that the cops are racist. That's not hard to understand. Most white people of the cops' social class are racists. Surely anthropologists recognize that. But cops want respect, and they're not getting it. They're uneducated. They may or may not be smart. Who can tell? They're inarticulate, but they sure as hell are aware of status. They hate it that college kids have money, so they grab this opportunity to beat them up. Maybe those college wiseasses will someday become doctors and lawyers and live in the suburbs, but for right now they're going to get their heads cracked. It's class warfare. Not quite the kind Marx had in mind, maybe, but class conflict nonetheless. The police have never read Marx or Weber or much of anything else, but they sure understand social hierarchy. They've internalized it."

Liz did not respond directly. "It was remarkable that nobody shot police. That's going to start now, I think. It would be suicide, of course."

Bill slowed the car for a residential area. "Some of the people in the movement—not many, I hope, but some—are cases of what the police call 'suicide by cop'. Those people don't expect to win, and they know there's at least great risk that they'll be severely punished, maybe even killed. But they don't value their lives very much. Some of them think they deserve to be punished. Some don't want to live. There are different degrees of despair."

Six

Nov. 3, 1969, Ann Arbor, the apartment

Bill picked up a pair of Liz's blue jeans from the floor and hung them on a hook on the bedroom wall.

Liz was reading, but she watched him do it. Then she said, "You know, it's a small thing, but it annoys me when you pick up after me. It's a criticism."

"Not a direct one."

"No, an implied one, which is worse."

"I don't understand why you would just drop clothes on the floor and leave them."

"Because it's a bother to pick them up. I thought that was obvious."

"Not much bother."

She put down the book. "It's interesting. You place a very high value on the maintenance of order. That puzzles me. It's surprising that someone who is so fond of order would embrace a revolutionary cause."

Bill paused. "Some things are more important than order."

151

"Yes, they are. But I'm a student of culture. These value systems usually go together. They come in bundles."

"You attach too much weight to small customs."

"Uh huh. Maybe I'll start hanging up your clothes."

"You won't find them on the floor. You'll have to take them off me first."

November 12, 1969, District of Columbia, and Langley, Virginia

Bill received a summons from Rabbit and had to report to Langley two days later. He told Liz that he was going to visit family.

At the end of their meeting, Rabbit issued an invitation. "Bill, you're lucky. While you're in DC, an old friend of mine, Earl Hines, will be in town. He's going to come over to my place tonight for a social occasion, some informal music. I've invited a few friends to stop by to hear him. You'd be most welcome to join us."

"The great Earl Hines?"

"That's the one."

"I'll be there with bells on."

"Kill the bells."

"Should I wear my new suit?"

"It wouldn't hurt."

"Right. Thanks, Rabbit."

Rabbit's home

Rabbit lived in a limestone co-op building in the Kalorama Triangle, near Rock Creek Park. The Taft Bridge on Connecticut Avenue, conveniently nearby, spans a deep gorge made by Rock Creek, and the bridge was reputed to have been used by the Agency for cases that were "terminated with extreme prejudice." The stories led to good-natured joshing. Rabbit's friends sometimes said that he lived close to his work.

The door of the apartment was opened by a slender, elegant black man wearing a white jacket, crisply pressed gray trousers, and highly polished shoes. Rabbit told Bill later that the man's name was George Washington. There were many Washingtons among the black residents of the District. The apartment was much as Bill had expected—there were oriental rugs, good Caucasian ones, mahogany furniture, some with inlay of other woods, silver tea services, and so on. It was rather fussy, not to Bill's taste, but clearly grand. Bill didn't recognize the artists on the walls.

Earl Hines had brought with him a young saxophone player from Chicago. They planned to improvise some duets. There was no bass or drums. Bill took Rabbit aside and said, "I think it would be better if I avoid the Chicago guy. He might know some of the Ann Arbor people, who are about his age. Chicago is a big feeder to the University."

Rabbit said, "Good point. We won't mention your saxophone days, or even your knowledge of jazz. Just enjoy the music."

About twenty guests were present. There was a grand piano at one end of the living room and chairs had been arranged facing it. It was not a dinner party. It was what, at another time or place, might have been called a musicale or at still another time might have been a jam session.

Before the music started, a handsome woman in her early sixties came over and introduced herself to Bill. She had pure white hair and wore a deep red dress. She also wore pearls. "I'm Penny Maranville, Rabbit's wife. You must be Bill Burke."

"That I am, Mrs. Maranville. Thank you very much for inviting me."

At that point, Rabbit came over. "I was about to introduce you, Penelope, but I see you've met Bill."

She said, "Charles, where have you been hiding this beautiful young man?"

Rabbit turned to Bill, "She calls me Charles to punish me for calling her Penelope." And then, to her, "I've been hiding him at the office. He's an absolute whiz at selling hailstorm insurance to elderly widows."

They both laughed, so Bill joined them.

The music was fine. Hines was a phenomenon. He was clearly elderly (his hair was not his own), but he played with precision, lyricism, and imagination. In the 1920s, when he worked with Louis Armstrong, Hines was influential in changing the way that jazz piano was played. He introduced what became known as "trumpet style" piano.

When the music had concluded, a *grande dame* of Washington society complimented the musicians. "Mr. Hines, I saw your father play at the Grand Terrace in Chicago, almost forty years ago."

Hines replied, "Thank you, madam, but that wasn't my father.

That was me and it was at least forty years ago. But they used to call me 'Father Hines.'"

She said, "Oh, my."

The next day, Rabbit's office

"That was wonderful music last night. Thanks for inviting me."

"I'm glad you enjoyed it. Earl is always in top form. He likes to have an audience that doesn't talk during the music." Rabbit leaned back in his desk chair and looked at Bill across the top of his reading glasses. "You and I both played jazz—even the same songs. Maybe in somewhat different styles, but not too far apart. You played saxophone; I played piano. That's probably not a significant difference, but we are different people. And it's not just a matter of age." He picked up a pipe and appeared to consider it. "I didn't have the benefit, as you did, of going to our government-funded finishing school. I didn't learn how to kill people. Not my thing. I was a lawyer as much as a jazz pianist—a friend of both Adlai Stevenson and Benny Goodman, Eddie Condon and Whitney North Seymour—a charming mixture of the respectable and the raffish, an ever-so-slightly daring Episcopalian".

Maranville smoked a corncob pipe, the sort smoked by General Douglas MacArthur. Bill thought that perhaps Rabbit was a MacArthur admirer. That would make some sense. As he toyed with the pipe, filling it, tamping down the tobacco, lighting it, re-lighting it, he would sometimes point the stem toward the window and move it in small, complex patterns, arabesques. This puzzled Bill, but he finally decoded it. The tip of the stem was writing "Maranville." Bill never told Rabbit that he had figured it out.

Having dealt with the pipe, Rabbit spoke again. "Who are these kids? What are their goals? How do they think? If we want to prevent trouble, and we surely do, then we need to get inside their heads. Their arguments are stated in more-or-less rational terms. Some of the arguments are better formulated, more articulate, more cogent, more persuasive. Others are garbage. Nonetheless, they're attempts at rational argument. But what's really going on, underneath, is an adventure, romance, a quest for power, the thrill of risk. They want some excitement in their lives. Most of them aren't looking forward to sitting at a desk in the family canned goods business, making telephone calls, sending out invoices, making deals on the golf course. But now they're adults — sort of — and they want to do things they call 'meaningful.' They aren't always sure what the meaning is of meaningful, but it always has something to do with making a better world. Fine. That's all to the good. Are they naïve? Sure. They say they realize that someone is likely to get hurt in the struggle. But that's abstract. It hasn't happened yet, or not much. So they can advocate violence without feeling the pain. Or, they can advocate it until they feel the pain."

Bill shifted in his chair, uncomfortably. "I think these students, some of them thirty years old by the way, older than I am, are more serious than you give them credit for. Some of them, at least, are conscious that revolution can be a romantic fantasy. I've heard them say that they don't want to play at being pirates or cowboys. But they don't like the world they see or the government they see, and they don't want to accept it. They want to fight injustice."

Rabbit looked at the ceiling. "The kids in the ghetto get in trouble, too, basically because of the same impulses and secretions. Kids get in trouble. It's what they do." He relighted the pipe. "Maturity comes sooner to some than to others."

"That's true, but it's not just a matter of maturity. There are different goals, different tastes for risk, different levels of tolerance for injustice. If maturity is defined as giving up, they aren't there yet."

"Well, whatever their tastes, we need to know what they're planning if it presents a threat. And, if it does, we need to act to shut it down. It's one thing to understand them, it's another to sympathize."

"Detachment while participating is a nice trick."

"No doubt. But that's what makes a good agent. Speaking of detachment, I don't want you sleeping with Liz."

Bill stood, looked at Rabbit, and walked to the window. "She's interested in sex, Rabbit. Is that so difficult to understand? It's a normal thing. If I walk away from her, I'll lose my best source about what's going on in the Weathermen and I'll lose any influence on their future plans. I also don't want to, personally."

"I think this is affecting your judgment. Liz's friends are more dangerous than you give them credit for. I've been in this business a long time. I've seen young agents come and go. I've seen them make mistakes. My experience tells me you're making a mistake."

Bill unconsciously clenched his fists, and he consciously decided not to suppress his anger. If his personal life compromised his cover identity, that would be a legitimate concern of the CIA.

But fucking didn't do that. If anything, it reinforced his cover. Rabbit could piss up a rope. Bill walked toward the door. "Sex is a normal thing, Rabbit. Think back. It's what people do when they're in love with each other. You get to give pleasure to each other. Try to remember. I wouldn't have taken you for a puritan. You're willing to kill in defense of this country, but you're not willing to use sex out of wedlock?"

"Careful, Bill. That's not the issue, and you know it." Rabbit took a file folder from the table behind his desk. "Is the relationship instrumental or is it emotional?"

Bill paused before responding. "It's both."

"That's the problem." He put the file back on the table. "Are you resigning?"

"No, I'm not. You need me."

December 4-6, 1969, Ann Arbor

The death of Fred Hampton, the chairman of the Black Panther Party in Illinois, was a hot topic at the Voice bar. Hampton had been killed when fourteen policemen assigned to the office of the Cook County State's Attorney entered the Panthers' apartment at 4:30 a.m. while Hampton was sleeping. Gunfire resulted. How many shots were fired and by whom were contested matters. Another Panther, Matt Clark, was also dead, and four members of the Party were in the hospital. All of the Panther survivors who had been in the apartment during the raid were charged with attempted murder and armed violence.

When news of Hampton's death reached the bar, the story

was the account given by the State's Attorney at a press conference, that an attempt to serve a search warrant was met with gunfire from the Panthers. But this was soon disputed. The Panthers said that the police came in shooting. It was uncontested that Hampton died on his bed. As the Panthers had it, he was executed, murdered while he slept. They said he didn't wake when the shooting started and must have been drugged by a government agent, a traitor.

Hal said, "This is war. Chicago has just declared all-out war on black people and on political parties it doesn't like. The message is clear: 'Fuck around with us and we'll kill you.' Are we going to let this go?"

Liz said, "How do we fight it?"

Hal was quick, "Shoot back."

Bill was cautious, "They have more guns than we do, and bigger ones."

Hal's voice was calm. "Next time we're in a situation where a cop is facing a crowd of people, there should be a shot from somewhere in that crowd that snuffs the cop. There'd be no way to prove who fired the shot."

Bill said, "Yeah, that's a good plan, except that half of the people in the crowd would be police informants."

Hal again. "You should know."

Bill stood, walked to Hal's table, and looked down at him. "What the hell's that supposed to mean?"

Hal squirmed. "You played cop in Chicago, right?"

Bill put on his coat. "I've had enough of this bullshit. I'm going out for some air."

After Bill had left, Jim Mellor said, "Some people do a lot of talking about offing the pigs, but Willy is the only guy we have here who has actually beat up a cop. Chicago has a warrant on him for aggravated assault."

BJ said, "Yeah, the cop knocked Liz down and Willy was angry."

Liz said, "The cop didn't really knock me down. I slipped. But then he took a swing at Willy."

Mellor replied, "Watch out when Willy is angry."

Hal put his own spin on it. "I think Willy was a professional fighter. Was he in Special Forces or a martial arts guy?"

Mellor said, "Don't know. Don't know much about him really except that Liz likes him."

Liz stood up. "Yeah, sure do. He wasn't in the military by the way. He had deferments until he passed age twenty-six."

The next day, the conversation at the bar resumed. There was new information from Chicago. Mellor had talked to one of his college classmates, a criminal lawyer.

He said, "Skip Wendell tells me that the cop version of the Hampton raid is bullshit. After the surviving Panthers were all in custody, but while a few were still in the apartment, one of the cops went into Hampton's bedroom and fired two shots into his head from close range. Hampton was already wounded or unconscious on his bed."

Bill said, "The forensic evidence should show if he was shot at close range. It's hard to know how the cops thought they could get away with it."

Mellor replied. "Yeah, unless they deliberately screw up the evidence. Maybe Hampton's head gets damaged in autopsy, or maybe the mattress or the bed gets moved so the angles are different, so you can't reach conclusions. Skip removed a door from the apartment and took it home with him because it shows that the bullets were coming from the outside of the apartment, going in, not from the inside going out, and he's afraid that the cops will destroy the evidence."

Hal asked, "Who's Skip?"

"He's a lawyer who represents some of the Panther survivors. A friend of mine."

Bill asked, "If the place is a murder scene, can he take the door?"

"I don't know, but he did. Skip has guts."

Liz asked, "Did the Panthers have guns?"

Mellor replied, "Sure they had guns, but the question is whether they used them, or who shot first. Skip says the cops were armed with a Thompson submachine gun, a carbine, several shotguns—some of them police issue and some private weapons—and numerous pistols. Fourteen cops with all those weapons. That's a hell of a lot of firepower for serving a search warrant. It was a search and destroy mission, mostly destroy."

Bill said, "Again, the ballistics evidence should show that the cops did the shooting."

Mellor went to the heart of it. "Yeah, but who's going to prosecute them? They're the State's Attorney's cops. He's the prosecutor—who is going to bring the charges? And who is a jury or a judge going to believe, or pretend to believe?"

BJ spoke. "I'm from Chicago. It'll be handled in the same way that all other Chicago investigations into police conduct are handled—with professionalism—that is, with complete, utter, unvarnished, bald-faced lies. The Chicago police are as crooked as a dog's hind leg. And considerably more vicious than that dog. There's a real irony here. Bill Bissell urged Fred Hampton to have the Panthers join us in the National Action, the so-called Days of Rage, and Hampton replied, 'If we did anything like that, they'd just shoot us.'"

Liz said in a cold, quiet voice, "This country is even worse than I thought. The fundamental corruption, fundamental inhumanity, is sickening. Unbelievable."

BJ replied, "Read history."

Hal returned to his theme. "They did this at 4:30 in the morning so there would be no witnesses around. This was a hit squad. We're going to have to organize the same kind of thing."

December 18, 1969, the apartment

Bill was typing. He was writing a story about swimming in a creek, but he had yet to invent a client for whom the work was being done. The story was titled, straightforwardly, "Swimming in a Creek." Liz was late getting up this morning. The weather was gloomy. Small, widely-separated drops of rain were falling. As Bill closed the kitchen window, Liz emerged sleepily from the bedroom.

"Toast?" he asked.

"Sure."

"Tea?"

"Sounds good."

Bill said, "Okay. I'll boil. Black tea. No frou-frou teas, no peppermint or clove nonsense."

She stretched. "Yeah, good. Two-fisted tough guy tea."

He went to the stove. "The kind that puts hair on your chest."

"I hope not."

After tending to the teapot, he said, "Isn't there supposed to be a national council meeting sometime soon? I think the major players are all out on bail now."

There may have been irony in that statement, but Liz didn't comment on it. "The national office didn't decide or at least didn't announce the time and place of the meeting until two days ago. I think they didn't want to attract unwanted visitors. Planning illegal actions would violate the terms of their bail, and mine, and we would all be arrested. The meeting is going to be in Flint in the week between Christmas and New Year's."

" A festive time of year. That should be cheery. Don't Weathermen have parents or brothers or sisters, nieces and nephews?"

"We're supposed to be committed to the cause. We *are* committed. We want attendance at the meeting to be selective—a meeting for people who are serious."

"Am I invited?"

"I'm not sure. There are some people who wouldn't want you there."

"Like Hal?"

"Hal certainly. Maybe also others."

"Why?"

"You make them uncomfortable. They doubt your commitment."

"Sorry to hear that." Bill pulled the toast out of the toaster and poured the tea. "Jam?" He looked at her. "What the hell is a woman doing wearing pajamas? I've never seen any sense in wearing pants while sleeping."

163

"Keeps your bottom warm."

"Put on a blanket."

"Not warm enough."

"Put on another blanket."

"Okay. I'll take them off."

"You're beautiful."

"Oh, you just like girls who aren't wearing any clothes."

"Only some of those girls," he said, grinning. "There is a certain appeal."

December 26, 1969, Flint

Liz's old VW beetle was still running. So long as there wasn't snow, they would be okay.

The Detroit collective was in charge of arrangements for the meeting and had rented an old dance hall in the poor, black center of Flint. The building looked as if it had seen better days, but perhaps there had never been good days. To welcome members to the meeting, Mark Rudd pointed to a large hole in the front door and told them that it had been caused by a shotgun blast the night before. It was true. A customer at a dance had been killed. A Christmas killing.

The decorations in the hall were elaborate and may have been intended to be a parody of Christmas. There were streamers and posters everywhere. Posters of Fidel Castro, Che Guevara, Eldridge Cleaver, Ho Chi Minh, Lenin, Mao, Malcolm X. One whole wall was covered with Fred Hampton. Some of the Hampton posters were on a red background, some on black. The colors alternated across the wall. Hanging from the ceiling, suspended on chains, was a six-foot long cardboard machine gun. The name of the meeting had been changed from the "National Council" to the "National War Council."

More than 300 people were present. Rudd and Meyer announced that there was "no set program" for the meeting. Instead, there would be speeches, free form debate, and karate exercises to prepare members for combat. A packet distributed by the national office said that "public violence is increasingly key."

Bill looked around the ballroom. "Some of those kids over there are thirteen or fourteen years old."

Liz nodded. "The national office is working on recruiting high school kids."

Bill said, "Jesus!" He went in search of a can of beer. Drugs were plentiful but beer was scarce.

Then speeches started, and the speakers relentlessly pursued the theme of the meeting. There were repeated calls for "armed struggle." One man said, "We will burn and loot and destroy." Another said that he was "determined to destroy the state." These sentiments were milder than some. It appeared that each speaker was trying to top the previous promise, upping the ante.

Bill was happier when the karate exercises started. Jim Mellor, who was a big guy, assembled a group of enthusiasts and began to instruct them in the moves. He wasn't very good at it. The pupils were told to form pairs for the purpose of practicing on each other. This wasn't organized, and the pairing took some time. Bill offered Hal the opportunity to practice on him, but Hal declined.

When they began trying out the moves, Bill had fun, but he had to restrain himself. He was too good. It was obvious that he knew what he was doing. "Yeah, well, I was in the karate club in high school." Jim tried to get him to help instruct, but Bill was modest. "I'm not that good."

He wasn't going to let people hit him, however. He blocked every blow they threw. He tried to specialize in instructing Liz, in order to protect her, but she wouldn't let him do that. He had to be careful not to hurt people. After half an hour of continuous exercise, he took a break. He went over to the sideline and drank from a can of Bud.

Liz said, "You look good out there."

He replied, "Just natural talent, Babe."

When he went back out on the practice floor, at first he continued to block all moves. But then he started missing. He got hit. His timing seemed to be off. He became awkward. Someone took him down with a throw. Bill picked himself up, stood, but looked confused. He thought the room was getting dark. He tried to focus. He had to breathe, had to think about breathing; he needed to remember that. Had he lost his wallet again? Why would they hold a party in a place that doesn't have any lights? Someone challenged him, but he didn't respond.

Liz came over. "Are you okay?"

"I want to rest." Then he collapsed onto the floor.

Kathy Boudin ran to help.

Liz shouted, "Willy, are you okay?"

He said, weakly, "Drugs."

Kathy asked, "Does he do drugs?"

Liz said, "No. He won't touch them."

Jim Mellor and Kathy Boudin supported Bill and got him to the parking lot while Liz went to get the VW. By now, he couldn't speak, or perhaps he was still conscious enough to realize that he shouldn't speak. Jim, Kathy, and Liz put Bill into the passenger seat and laid him as flat as possible, mostly on the seat, but partly on the floor. One of the police cars watching the dance hall gave her an escort to the nearest emergency room. The cop used his siren to get them through red lights. The hospital was supposed to be only a few minutes away, but to Liz it seemed longer. By the time they reached the hospital, Bill was unconscious.

He was taken inside on a gurney and almost immediately given an injection by a nurse. He quickly revived. Liz then sat in the waiting room for three hours while Bill was kept under observation and his vital signs were taken. Before he was released, Liz spoke to the doctor.

"What was it?"

"We can't be entirely sure without chemical analysis of his blood, but he had all the symptoms of a heavy dose of barbiturate."

"He doesn't do drugs. *Never.*"

"Well, he sure got hold of something. I smelled beer. He spit up some on his shirt."

"He was exercising and was thirsty. He drank about half a can of beer."

"Well, the drug could have been chloral hydrate, commonly known as 'knockout drops.' Nasty stuff. It could have been in the beer if someone was out to get him. If so, it's a damn good thing he didn't drink the whole can."

Liz took care of the paperwork for his release. Willy Feld didn't have health insurance. He was a freelance ghostwriter and didn't have a regular employer, but Liz had a credit card. Her father would pay the medical bills.

Liz brought the beetle to the front door of the hospital. A wheelchair was provided to get Bill to the car, but he refused it. He stood and pushed the chair to the front door. Liz drove back to Ann Arbor. They did not return to the National War Council, and they didn't talk much in the car.

January 3, 1970, Ann Arbor

Bill reported to Rabbit about the Weatherman assembly at Flint and his trip to the hospital.

"The bastards drugged me. The clumsy jackasses were trying to learn karate, and I was trying hard not to hurt them. We took a break and I took a couple of swigs from a can of beer, and a couple of minutes later I passed out. Liz got me to a hospital."

"Do they know who you are?"

"No, I don't think so, or else they would have denounced me and maybe beaten me up. I think they, or maybe only one guy, wanted to get rid of me, to get me out of the meeting."

"Would that be the guy who is jealous of your relationship with Liz?"

"It could be. You're very well-informed."

"I try to be. It's my job. Did he want to kill you?"

"Probably not. He just wanted me gone. He's a bit nuts, but he's not that nuts."

"Are you sure?"

"How can you ever be sure? He's certainly had plenty of opportunities. I think he's just jealous. But it could be somebody else. A lot of them are devious."

Rabbit paused. "It's a bad situation. I don't like it."

"I didn't much like it either."

"What did the hospital have to do to revive you?"

"I think they just gave me an injection of a stimulant, probably epinephrine. The doctor told Liz that the drug that knocked me out was maybe chloral hydrate."

"We should pull you."

"Don't do that. I'm okay now, and the strategic situation is getting a lot more dangerous. Weatherman is dividing up into cells and going underground. They decided on that at Flint after Liz and I left the meeting. That may be why they didn't want me there, but I've picked up the talk. Unless you've got somebody else in close, you need me to track this. They're going underground because they're planning serious violence, bombings."

"Okay. We need you. We'll leave you in place for now, but stay in frequent contact with me, and be careful about these calls. They know how to tap wires. And watch what you drink."

"Got it. Will do."

January 10, 1970, Ann Arbor

Many of the afternoons at the bar were now slow, and this was one of them. Liz had time to read. But then BJ came in. He sat at the bar and ordered a cup of coffee.

Liz said, "I'll make some."

BJ waved a hand. "Don't bother."

"No bother. I need to make some for other customers." She filled the percolator with water. "Don't you drink beer?"

169

"I drink beer, just not very often and not very much. And never spirits." BJ then recited, "'Never support two weaknesses at the same time. It's your combination sinners who dishonor the vices and bring them into bad repute.'"

Liz laughed.

BJ disclaimed authorship: "That's from Thornton Wilder, 'Our Town,' a play."

"I've never seen it." Liz finished making the coffee.

"It's a good one."

The coffee perked.

As BJ drank his coffee, Liz said, "I need advice."

"Sure. Shoot."

"I'm uncertain or undecided on what I should do. The split in SDS is causing trouble. Like other people, I suppose, I'm pulled in two directions. In my case, especially, Willy is pulling one way and Hal is pulling the other. I certainly want the government to change. I'm sure about that. I'm sickened by Vietnam. But I'm not sure a violent strategy will help. As you know, some of our friends are talking about bombs, and I think they mean it. How do you know whether you're doing the right thing?"

"I assume you're not asking me about how to choose between Willy and Hal. I can't tell you about that."

"No. You can let me handle that part of it. But what is the right political choice, the moral choice?"

"I think we usually judge or decide such things by how we feel about what we're doing, by whether we feel good about it. What are you comfortable with? Follow your heart."

"But the heart changes. Some days one way; on another day, a different feeling."

"Yes, the heart changes and the heart can make mistakes, but sometimes you get it right and a light dawns. Even then, you might not see the answer clearly. It's hard to be sure. We need to be honest with ourselves. Later, of course, your mistakes or failures become clear—your successes not so much so." BJ took his coffee cup from the bar and moved to a table. He settled in. "In discussions of this issue, I hear some standard arguments. There are a bunch of clichés. Radicals trot out the forest fire that gets rid of weed trees and renews the forest, and then there's the necessity for surgery to cut the cancer out of the body. On the other side, conservatives ask 'what trees do they plant?' But none of that talk gets us very far. These are false analogies."

"So what should I do?"

"A religious person would tell you to pray for guidance. Some of the people in the peace movement answer the question that way."

"Do you?"

"No." BJ stared into his coffee cup, as if looking for tea leaves. "This is a problem of ends and means. That is, as it is usually put, it is a question of whether the end justifies the means. There's no way to resolve that unless you can measure the weight or importance or value of both the end and the means, on the same scale. We don't have any way to do that. There are competing values here. Do we use a set of religious principles or some secular view of morality? So, I'm sorry, but I can't give you a clear answer. And sometimes we have to be, or ought to be, willing to act despite uncertainty. Follow your heart."

"Do you want some more coffee?"

"No, I don't want to become a caffeine addict, a combination sinner."

January 15, 1970, the apartment

There was snow on the ground. Both walking and driving were difficult, but Bill and Liz were tired of being cooped up inside. They needed groceries.

Bill said, "I'll go out and get us something to eat."

"That's a good idea. Make it starchy—maybe macaroni and cheese. I need comforting."

"I'll give you a backrub."

"Mac and cheese will work."

Bill went to the closet and got his winter jacket. "You seem depressed lately. Can I help?"

Liz got up from the sofa, walked to Bill, and kissed him on the cheek. "Is this a good time to talk?"

"Sure. Why not?" Bill shrugged.

Liz went to the kitchen table and picked up a mug. "I want to have friends, Willy. You're sweet, but you're basically a loner. You want to go your own way. You don't seem to like most of the people in Weatherman. You're driving my friends away. We need a group, a team to make a movement. We can't do it alone. I don't even want to try to do it alone. I like to work with other people, to share accomplishments. Is that a female thing? Is it more macho to work alone? To run through walls, overcome all obstacles, all by yourself? Is that so you can get all the credit? I don't need that."

Bill hung his jacket on a chair. "Would you like me to make coffee to put in the cup you're carrying around?" He paused. "I'm willing to work with other people when I think what they're doing makes sense, but I'm not willing to follow their lead when I think they're wrong, or crazy, or irresponsible. And you're right, I don't like some of the other guys here. It's hard to like guys who put knockout drops in your beer. Take Hal, for example. He's a jerk. You can see that! Jim Mellor is okay. I like him. BJ is smart and an interesting man, but he's a morphine addict. We don't have a lot in common. I'm not by nature a troublemaker I guess. But I don't think you are either."

Liz put the mug down. "There's more at stake here than small troubles or personal annoyance. I want to work for racial and economic justice. The assassination of Fred Hampton shows the truth about this country. The country is governed by force, and the response to that has to be force. Revolution is never quiet and peaceful, but I want to be part of it."

Bill stood by the window. "The new leadership, the gang that calls themselves the 'Weather Bureau', is trying to sell the line that the Days of Rage was a success, but it's hard to see how getting the crap beat out of you by the Chicago cops advances the cause. BJ, who is just as radical as the Bureau, sees it as the disaster it was. All it did was discredit the movement and make us look crazy and dumb. That's because the tactics in Chicago *were* crazy and dumb. And now the leadership wants to do more of that. That's bullshit. Breaking glass doesn't help. It's easy to break glass; it's a lot harder to change society."

"I agree. We have to break a lot more than glass."

Bill looked out the window. "Now it's raining. We'll have slush."

January 20, 1970, Ann Arbor

It was the middle of the morning, a cold day. Bill was working in the University's library and Liz had called Hal to arrange for him to meet her at the bar, which was closed in the morning. It wasn't doing much business since the split in SDS and the collapse of Voice. Hal knocked on the locked door, Liz opened it, and he came in quickly.

"Cold!," he said.

"Yeah, thanks for coming."

"Any time." He sat at a table.

"Can I get you something?"

"No thanks. I want to hear what's on your mind."

"I need to make a choice."

"We all do…. We all do." Hal took off his parka.

"It's tough. It isn't easy." Liz joined him at the table.

"What's so tough? Surely you don't want the country to keep going on the path it's on now."

"No, of course not, but the question is, how do we stop that."

"We have to take action, strong action, action that will change things."

"Like what?"

Hal said, "Bombings." Liz cringed. Hal answered the cringe, "You wanted an answer. I gave you an honest one."

"People will be killed?"

"Probably. I think it's inevitable. Richard Nixon will push us to that."

"I don't want to kill people."

"No." Hal changed course. "I don't want to either. And we all hope it won't come to that. Nobody wants that. But look at how many people are being killed in Vietnam and Cambodia now. We have a moral duty to stop the war if we possibly can. If we plan it right, we can destroy power plants, railroads, and bridges without killing people. Even occupied buildings are vacant a lot of the time. ROTC buildings on college campuses have been burned in the past year without killing anybody. When this country can no longer function, the voters will get tired of the war in Vietnam."

"I don't know ... I can't sleep. Willy argues that violent tactics will just turn people against us."

"Willy is a do-nothing. I'll bet he doesn't have any trouble sleeping. Right? You fuck and three minutes later he goes to sleep. Right?"

"You know, Hal, you can be an asshole. Is this really all about Willy?"

"I came here this morning because you asked me to. I came here to help."

"Yeah, you did, but it isn't helping."

"What do you want from me?"

She got up and walked behind the bar. "Sympathy. Advice. Understanding. What we should do isn't so clear. BJ told me to follow my heart, but that didn't help either. My heart isn't telling me what to do." To occupy her hands, Liz took a wet cloth and polished the bar. "This is a democracy. Maybe we should let the people decide."

Hal formed his words carefully. "The people are stupid. They don't read. They don't know what's going on, and they're conned by slick politicians, hucksters."

Liz turned on him and shouted, the bar forming a wall between them. "What should we call a movement that wants to seize power against the will of the majority, seizing that power through the use of force and violence? What should we call that? 'Dictatorship' sounds like the right word."

"Yes, the dictatorship of the proletariat."

"Ask the proletariat about that. They aren't buying it."

Hal stood up, but didn't move toward the bar. "Think about the French resistance during the German occupation. At first, the resistance just distributed anti-Nazi messages, and they weren't very effective. Most Frenchmen, in fact, cooperated with the Germans. But then the resistance started blowing things up and they crippled the German army. And when the resistance started winning, it became popular. Most people just support the winners. Yes, some of the resistance fighters were killed, many of them were, but in the end they won. The Germans were defeated. It was worth the sacrifice. You can't just do nothing. That's not a moral position."

"It's not a choice between doing something and doing nothing. Action just for the sake of taking action is pointless. In fact, some actions are worse than pointless. They're harmful. We all want our lives to count for something—sure, of course. The question is, how to do that."

Hal put on his parka. "Are demonstrations and marches a better strategy than bombs? Maybe they would be if we were permitted to have demonstrations and marches. But the Chicago cops and Richard Nixon and the FBI and the National Guard won't permit that. If your speeches start attracting a following, then the pigs will shoot you and kill you—like Dr. King and

Malcolm X and Bobby Kennedy and Fred Hampton. Then you won't demonstrate anymore, or march, or talk. How do you fight that?"

He went out the door.

Liz was angry. She didn't like Hal, but she thought he was mostly right. She didn't have an answer.

Seven

February 1, 1970, the apartment

Bill was in the bedroom and Liz was in the living room where she placed a phone call. She spoke softly, and she didn't think that Bill could hear her because he was sleeping. He stayed out of sight.

Bill could hear only Liz's side of the call, and even that he couldn't hear well. It was something about Madison, probably the University of Wisconsin. Then he heard the word "sterling." Bill knew that the Army Mathematics Research Center was in Sterling Hall at Wisconsin. There had been trouble there the year before. Liz's voice wasn't distinct, but she sounded excited or apprehensive or maybe frightened. She said, "Heavy stuff."

Bill waited fifteen minutes and then came out of the bedroom with tousled hair and rubbing his eyes. He engaged her in small talk. In the course of it, he said, "Wow! It's February. A whole month has passed since my adventures in Flint. It seems like only yesterday, my encounter with Mickey Finn."

"Mickey Finn?"

"Old movies nonsense. It means a drugged drink, without

178

the drinker knowing it." Then he abruptly changed the subject to avoid more talk about what happened in Flint. "February in Ann Arbor is cold."

Liz said, "Yes, and I'm going to have to be away for Valentine's Day. I'm sorry."

"Valentine's Day?"

"Yeah, Valentines. You know, hearts and flowers, the 14th."

"I'll miss you."

"I'm going to Chicago for a day or two to visit a friend. Girl stuff."

"That's cool. We'll make up for it."

Then he said, "How about take-out Chinese tonight?"

Liz wasn't enthusiastic. "Okay, if that's what you want."

Bill thought that he couldn't take the time required to access the secure line at Langley. He would have to call Rabbit at home. And he couldn't use the public phone at the gym. Hal might be on to it. Rabbit was right that tapping was easy. But he knew that there was a phone booth at the Cathay Gardens. It wasn't very private and it would be an open line, but a message needed to be sent.

At the restaurant, after ordering the take-out, he went into the phone booth, closed the door, and placed the call to Rabbit.

"This is Prez. It's a good thing I had a pocketful of quarters."

"Prez! Good to hear from you. How is the jazz world?"

"Busy, lots of action."

"Where are you playing?"

"I'm at home now, but I've got a gig coming up soon, on the 14th in Madison. There's going to be a big Valentine's Day dance at the University."

"Is it going to be ballads, or will it be rock and roll?"

"Rock, I'm afraid. Rock with a heavy backbeat."

"Will the full band be there?"

Bill moved closer to the wall where the telephone was mounted, so that there was less chance of being overheard. "I'm afraid so. My employers would like to have the bass section."

"Can I help?" Rabbit was cautious.

"It would be great if you could help me find some people who read music. Could you line up Sterling?"

"Sterling?"

"Yeah, Sterling would be great."

"Okay. Thanks Prez. I'll get on it."

The FBI picked up this conversation, probably from a tap on Rabbit's home phone, either in the constant search for moles or as a part of J. Edgar Hoover's campaign against the CIA. The monitor asked his superior, "What in the hell is this?"

"Oh, Maranville is a jazz musician. He's just fooling around with one of his buddies."

February 4, 1970, phone call

Once again Bill called Rabbit. He returned to the phone booth at the YMCA that he had used when he first came to Ann Arbor.

"The Weathermen have two cases of dynamite, fifty pounds each. They bought it in Keene, New Hampshire. They may have more."

"What are they going to do with it?"

"I don't know yet. I'm trying to find out. I think they plan to hit public buildings mostly, with a concentration on police stations and military stuff, including university buildings where military-funded research is going on. But they could, of course, also make anti-personnel devices."

"Is it going to Madison?"

"I don't think so. I think it's going to stay in the East. I can't ask."

"Where's the dynamite now?"

"Two guys went to New Hampshire. I'm not sure where they took it, but it probably went to New York City. I'm listening to chatter."

"Does Liz know where it is?"

"Maybe. Probably. I'm not sure. Liz and I are not getting along so well right now, and the Voice bar has closed. She lost her job. The split within SDS killed the bar. Too many fights, mostly verbal."

"So that means Liz is now your best source for finding out where the dynamite is and what the targets are."

"Yes, that's right, but she's become very cagey."

"Why?"

"I think some of the Weathermen have told her, clearly they have, that I'm a bad guy, maybe government."

"Does she believe it?"

"I think she doesn't want to believe it. Look, Rabbit, I want to try to save this girl, to save her life."

"Are you still intimate with her?"

"What? Intimate? How quaint!"

"You know what I'm asking and you haven't answered my question."

"I don't think I'm required to answer the question if you can't even say what you mean. But I'll tell you this. I have regard for Liz. I respect her. And she saved my ass when somebody drugged me. She's an intelligent and caring person. She's taken a moral position. She's being misled by charismatic assholes who live in a fantasy world, and she's participating in that fantasy, but the Weathermen promise solutions. The solutions are illusory, but the moral failings they address are real. You know as well as I that we're not covering ourselves with glory in Vietnam. Liz has made some bad decisions. Humans do that. She's human, Rabbit. She's a human life worth saving."

In a corner of Rabbit's office, there was an American flag on a pole. He had found that when he was concentrating on a difficult telephone call he tended to stare at the flag. It wasn't a conscious choice, but he was aware that he did it. Perhaps he hoped that the flag would remind him of his duty to the nation. "And if you save her life, how many more lives will be lost? That dynamite has the potential to kill dozens of people, scores. How many lives will you trade for hers?"

"I don't know. I don't know those people. I don't know what the circumstances will be. I don't know whether there'll be opportunities to save their lives. But I think I might be able to save hers. She's the decision we need to make now. She's the proximate problem."

"Then it's a very good thing that you aren't making that decision. It's my call. I'll take the responsibility. We need to find the dynamite. I want to let Liz Watson lead us to it. If you alert her, she'll bolt. You can't blow your cover. Don't warn her. Let her follow her own course. Let her lead us to it. I repeat: Don't interfere. I want to prevent the bombing. Period. Full stop."

182

"That's pretty calculating, Rabbit."

"Yes, I suppose it is. I suppose this job calls for a certain amount of calculation, even dispassion."

"I don't buy that."

"I see." Rabbit continued to stare at the flag. "And no doubt you feel that makes you a better person, one with finer sensibilities."

Bill hung up.

February 5, 1970, Ann Arbor

Bill went to a phone booth at the bus station at a prearranged time to receive a call from Rabbit.

"Bill, I want to see you. At my office."

"When?"

"Tuesday afternoon at four o'clock."

"I'll be there."

The same day, Bill and Liz, Ann Arbor,

Bill said, "I have to go out of town for a couple of days. I'll be back Wednesday or Thursday."

"Where are you going?"

"Family."

"Good family or bad family?"

"Bad."

"Short answer time, huh?"

"Yep."

February 10, 1970, Langley, Virginia

Bill and Rabbit were seated comfortably in Rabbit's office.

Rabbit said, "Here's what we know. We know that the Weatherman faction of SDS has a large amount of dynamite that they acquired in New Hampshire. We don't know much more than that, but they're obviously planning several bombings, or one damn big one. We need to track it, soon. We need to find the dynamite and find out what they plan to do with it."

Bill was straightforward. "I don't know where it went from New Hampshire, but I still think it went to New York City. And we don't know what they're planning, but a hundred pounds is enough to bring down a major bridge or destroy a hydroelectric dam if it's placed right. There's an instruction manual called 'The Blaster's Handbook'. It tells you how and where to place explosives if you want to bring down a building or whatever. I know the manual is in circulation among the Weathermen."

The afternoon sun was coming into the office and Rabbit turned in his chair to avoid it. "How'd they get their hands on that?"

"It's published by the International Society of Explosives Engineers. It's freely available. Dynamite has legitimate uses — that's a big part of the problem. We can shut down the New Hampshire source, but there are other ways to get dynamite. One is to steal it from coal mines, quarries, and construction sites. The most important thing about finding the dynamite is that it'll tell us who the dangerous guys are. The people who have it are the ones to watch."

"Agreed. So are you going to watch them?"

"I'm trying to track the dynamite that we know they already have. I could use some help with that. And, if we can find the stuff, we'll also find the guys who have it."

Rabbit knew that the president would be concerned about political fallout. "If you're going to investigate in New York, we're going to have to inform Nelson Rockefeller and the local police, and probably also the FBI."

Bill frowned. "We have to be careful. If the information about the dynamite is too specific, my cover will be blown. I don't know what they'd do then. I don't think they'd kill me, but I'm not sure about that. Drugging me at Flint suggests they're willing to play rough."

Rabbit took off his glasses. "I don't want to endanger you." He paused. "What are their motivations?"

Bill's pause matched Rabbit's. "I talk to people in the movement all the time. Without cross-examining them, I hope, I try to figure them out. But there's always a piece missing. I have the feeling I'm not getting something. There's a story they're not telling me, or maybe there's something they don't see about their own motives. They all say the same things — they condemn American racism, our imperialism in Vietnam, the suffering of the poor, and the evils of capitalism generally. They want to change things. I get that. But why they think they will be able to succeed with their tiny band of the faithful is a mystery."

"Perhaps you don't grasp it because you're not a man of faith."

"I'll give you that, I'm not, but I think there's more to it. These people are looking for something missing in their own lives, something they haven't found." Bill looked at Rabbit and smiled. "I think you said that to me once. Or something like it. What they're looking for is different for different people, of course. They've had different lives. Maybe if I knew them better I'd understand it."

"Or maybe not." Rabbit stood and moved to his desk. "Are you still seeing Liz?"

"Sure I'm seeing her. She's my primary source. Without her I don't have credibility."

"My sources tell me that you're living with her."

"Who tells you that?"

"This is the CIA, for Christ's sake. We have resources. Answer my question."

"This is inhuman, Rabbit."

Rabbit stood. "It's late in the day."

Bill remained seated. "Not very late."

"Yes it is. It's late in the day." Rabbit opened a locked cabinet behind his desk and took out a bottle of scotch. "Would you like a drink, Bill?" He produced two short glasses.

"Sure. I'll join you."

"Ice? Peanuts?"

"Yeah. You have everything."

"This is the CIA, as I said before. There's a peanuts line item in the dark budget. Tell me more about the Weatherman leader who has a drug vulnerability. Maybe we could use that."

"Okay. First, he's smart. He was doing a Ph.D. in philosophy when he decided to pursue revolution. He's still a graduate teaching assistant, paid less than your peanuts budget. He's charismatic, a leader. The other honchos like him. I like him. He's a little pedantic, but he's polite, he's charming, and he's a junkie."

"Oh for the good old days, when religion was the opiate of the people. What does he use?"

"Morphine. He has a woman friend at a hospital."

"What would happen if we got rid of his connection, cut off his supply?"

"He'd probably find another. If he didn't, he'd be in pain. But I don't see how that would help us. He might not be able to function for a time, and that might be a little disruptive in the organization, but it isn't going to change anything. It might lead to dumb decisions, I suppose."

"Would it make his team less effective, make their attacks less well-planned?"

"I doubt it. He's an inspirational leader, but he's not the nuts-and-bolts organizer."

"Who is?"

"There are three or four, I think. I'm not close enough to be sure."

"Why not?"

"They don't trust me. I think that's why they got rid of me at the Flint meeting. Most of my information comes from Liz."

Rabbit walked over to the window and ruffled the flag. "I'd like to enhance your Weatherman credibility, but we can't have you making bombs." Rabbit returned to his desk and sat on the edge of it. "There's a certain sort of artistic sensibility that seems to think morphine is romantic, or that taking opiates demon-strates that one's perceptions are so fine, so heightened, that it's necessary to dull them, to suppress them. We all know the

history: Edgar Allen Poe used opium, so did Coleridge. Tou-
louse-Lautrec had his absinthe, Van Gogh cut his ear off, but he
was probably just nuts, Cocteau was an opium addict, and legions
of writers have been drunks. I don't really see the attraction of it.
Or is it just a matter of being a member of that club?" He looked
at Bill. "Then again, I don't suppose they'd see the attraction of
being a bureaucrat."

"Poe wasn't an addict. That was a story made up by an enemy.
And all those artists you're talking about did good work, except
for some of the drunken writers."

Rabbit looked at the flag. "Do you still play the saxophone?"

Bill's handful of peanuts stopped halfway to his mouth. "No,
I haven't played in four or five years. I sold the horn when I was
in college and needed a new bicycle to get around the campus."

"That's just as well. My observation is that the sax is an un-
healthy instrument."

"Why do you say that?"

"Consider the evidence, Charlie Parker, Stan Getz, Art Pepper, and many others. It appears to be a requirement that to be
a bigtime saxophonist you have to be a heroin addict. What is it
with the sax?"

Bill raised to eye level his scotch on the rocks. "Chet Baker
and Miles Davis manage to consume heroin without playing the
sax, and I don't think Bud Freeman or the other earlier sax players
used smack, so far as I know."

"I wonder whether it was simply Parker's influence. He was
such a towering figure that the others emulated him."

"Maybe. The earlier guys—Freeman, Coleman Hawkins,
Ben Webster—were around before the contagion."

"The temptation, of course, is always to emulate the towering figures. I find the tendency holds even in other lines of endeavor. Even perhaps in our work. There are many types of human frailty—drugs, greed, fanaticism, lust, cowardice, dishonesty, self-regard, arrogance. And then there is the matter of loyalty, or the lack thereof. I don't mean to be running through the seven deadly sins. I have the particular situation before us more specifically in mind. And even without a serious character flaw, of course, people make bad choices. I see that in politics often. I'm sure you do, too. But it's harder to recognize it in ourselves. Whatever their motivations, or ours, there's personal responsibility. If people intend to do harm, we have to stop them, and that's our responsibility."

"That sounds like a sermon."

"Too damn bad. It's what I believe. Just be careful, Bill. Just be careful." Throughout the conversation, Rabbit had kept his eyes fixed on the flag.

Bill noticed that. "Your flag looks a bit tired, Rabbit. It's limp, faded. It's too near the window. It can't take the exposure to sunlight."

"I appreciate your concern for the flag." Rabbit opened a file folder on his desk. "Just so you'll have your eyes open, you have a need to know that BJ's woman friend at the hospital is our friend. I'm going to cut off the morphine supply. That may provoke a crisis, so be alert. We're done now, Bill."

Two days later, Ann Arbor

"Outside the Weather, people call me Bill, not Willy."

Liz stopped, put her head down. "And what last name?"

"Burke." For some perverse reason, Bill thought he should try to defend himself, but he knew it wasn't a good strategy. "I told you early on that Feld wasn't my real name."

"Yeah, but you said your grandfather changed it."

"That wasn't true."

"You mean it was a lie, like a lot about you, I think." Liz's eyes filled with tears of sadness, anger, and frustration. In a choked voice she said, "What are you? FBI?"

"No, not FBI. But I want you to know that I love you, Liz. That's real."

"Sure. Not FBI. Then what the fuck are you?"

"I can't say."

"Horseshit! You sure as fuck can say. You owe me at least that."

Bill had thought, hoped, that, if necessary, he could use the CIA to frighten Liz or at least give her pause. If she knew that the CIA was watching, maybe the Weathermen would change their plans.

"CIA. But as of now, I'm not CIA anymore."

"CIA? This is the United States. What the hell are you doing here?"

"The Vietnam war."

"This isn't Vietnam, you sonofabitch."

"It might as well be."

"What in the hell does that mean?"

"The SDS talked about bringing the war home. It succeeded.

The war's being fought here." He reached for her hand. She pulled away. "But I *do* love you, Liz. I won't do anything to hurt you."

"You already have, you dumb blind bastard. Go away! Get away from me. Now."

"I love you."

"You've said that, for what that's worth." She took three steps away, then turned. "You say the war's being fought here. You just wait and see."

"Do you want to kill people?"

"Do *you* want to? How many people are being killed in Vietnam?"

"The CIA knows about the dynamite you bought in New Hampshire, and they also know about Sterling Hall at the University of Wisconsin."

February 13, 1970, phone call

Bill made the difficult call to Rabbit from a phone booth at the Student Union.

"I talked to Liz. I told her I was CIA, I put it in the past tense, and I told her that I knew about the dynamite and about Sterling Hall in Madison. I intended to warn her. I hoped, I still hope, that she'll tell the others and they'll call it off, abandon whatever plans they might have. She didn't take it well. She accused me of betraying her, which, of course, I had. The only thing that seemed clear to her was that she couldn't trust me. She left, both crying and furious. And now I've lost track of her. I don't know where she is. I don't know what she'll do."

"That was damn stupid, Bill. First of all, I hope you realize that you are in great personal danger."

"I'm being careful. But you're right."

"I'm not worried about only you. If she talks, she could do considerable damage to the Agency. We're not supposed to be involved in domestic politics. But we need to keep the lid on, preserve the orderly functioning of government. The FBI is incompetent. If we simply fed information to them, they'd screw it up. And they don't talk to us." He paused. "We're way beyond public relations here. Violence is hurting the whole country, not just individual victims. But that rationale isn't going to mollify the FBI or the local police. They'll certainly say we were trespassing on their turf. There'll be congressional hearings. I'll be hung out to dry, and so will you."

"I don't care whether I'm hung out to dry. But you're in a political job, Rabbit. I can't control that. I can only do what I'm able to do. I just don't want Liz, or anyone, to die. I don't know whether she'll talk. She certainly knows that talking would endanger me. I don't think she's angry enough to do that. But she might be. But she's a good person."

"You had better damn well hope she keeps her mouth shut. I certainly do. I assume you know you are done here, whether you intended that or not."

"Yes. Goodbye, Rabbit."

February 14, 1970, Liz and Hal

After two days in a Holiday Inn, Liz called Hal and they met at

the Busy Bee Bakery. She needed something to eat. Over dough-
nuts, they spoke quietly.

Hal said, "I think I could find somebody who could beat the
crap out of him."

"No, don't."

"I wish I could do it myself but I don't think that's realistic."
He took a ferocious bite out of a doughnut. "We should probably
do more than just beat him up."

"No, no violence. I loved him. I hate him now, or at least I
think I do, but I loved him once. He was a fake, but he was good
to me. Don't hurt him."

"He's a trained assassin, Liz."

"Oh, I don't think so. He's just a guy who did a job, a nasty
job, but he got out of college looking for work and this is the job
he found. He was good at it."

"He lied to you."

"Sure. He had to. That was part of the job. I don't think he
wanted to. He didn't have to tell me who he was. He could've
continued to be a spy. I was very angry at him at first and I'm
still angry, and hurt, but now I realize that he gave something
up for me. He gave up his career. I think he did that because
he was trying to help me. I've thought about it. He was afraid I
was in danger — not an unreasonable fear — and he was trying
to protect me." Liz looked down. "I didn't give anything up for
him."

Hal slammed his hand flat on the table. Heads turned in the
bakery. "No, you didn't. You didn't give up your principles. You
were trying to make the world better. The only people he was
trying to protect were the fat cats, the oil companies. He's a fas-

193

cist, a sonofabitch. He doesn't deserve your…What is it? Not sympathy, surely. Consideration? I sure as hell hope it's not love."

"No, not love. Not now. But I don't think he's really evil. Wrong, but not evil."

"Well, then,…"

"Well, I want to leave. I need to get out of here."

"That's a good idea. I'll go with you. I'll help you."

"I don't want another boyfriend. Not yet."

"That's okay, Liz. I understand. Do you want another doughnut?"

"No, no doughnut either, but maybe another cup of coffee."

Hal went over to the counter and refilled their cups. "We could meet up with some of our friends, maybe in a big city where it'll be hard for him to find us. We can connect with the underground."

"Yeah, don't worry. I'll perk up pretty soon."

February 15, 1970, University of Michigan

Bill went to BJ's study in the library.

"Are you busy?"

"I don't want to talk to you." BJ continued looking at a book.

"I'm sorry to hear that."

BJ pushed his chair back but did not invite Bill to sit down. "Our friends tell me that you're a bad guy."

"They're right. But I'm trying to find Liz because I'm afraid she's going to get hurt."

"Are you going to offer to restore my morphine supply?"

"No, I'm not. What are you talking about?"

"Some idiot came here, sent by your employers, I assume, and he offered to get morphine for me if I would tell him where the dynamite is."

"Jesus!"

"The government is not only unprincipled but stupid. I hope the people who organized that are not the same people you work for. First they cut off my connection; they sent her out of state. Then they assume that I can't figure out how to get the stuff. It took me about twenty-four hours to find a new source of supply. It's only the government who can't find drugs. That's because their agents take bribes. Do you take bribes, Mr. X? I'm told that Willy isn't your real name."

"I'm Bill. I'm worried about Liz. She's disappeared. She's gone off somewhere, probably with Hal Roberts. He's gone, too. Hal is bad news, a hotdog. There's a lot of talk about bombs."

"I don't want to help you. You're a liar, among other things, but I like Liz and I don't want to see her get hurt."

"Her getting hurt is the important part of that. I don't ask that you like me, BJ. I'm sure you don't approve of what I did. I'm not sure I approve of it. But maybe I could find her and try to save her. Do you know where they've gone?"

"What if Liz doesn't want to be found? Why should I cooperate in your attempt to interfere? She's decided how she wants to live her life. Why shouldn't she have that freedom?" BJ put on his glasses.

Bill said, "I'm not taking any freedom away from her. I simply want to talk to her. She'll still do what she wants to do."

"But you work for the CIA. You'll blow the whistle on her, tell your employers where she is."

"No, I won't. I don't work for the CIA anymore, and I love Liz."

"Love is one thing. Duty is another. What's your duty to Liz? Do you have a duty to respect her freedom? She and her friends have obviously chosen to go underground in order to pursue a political cause, a cause that has very considerable merit. Yes, it may be dangerous, but it's their lives."

"Look, damn it, this isn't an exercise in sophistry. I don't want to approach this like a philosopher, I want to approach it as a human being. If someone you love was attempting suicide, would you really stand by and watch and just say, 'well, it's her choice'?"

"I'm not persuaded that this is a case of suicide, but I agree that there's a serious risk that she'll be hurt. I won't give you any real information—I don't have any—but I'll tell you how I would think about it. I'd bet on New York City. Hal would fit in there. You're right about him being a hotdog. He's tight with Hannah Meyer and the Columbia University crowd, Mark Rudd and so on. They'll know all the hiding places in New York. Chicago's another possibility, of course, but it's Weather Bureau headquarters and the Chicago cops are all over the Weathermen. They'll be looking for them there, so Liz and Hal will probably steer clear of it. Too hot. Some place like the Upper Peninsula has lots of isolated cabins, the classic hideout, but a bunch of twenty-somethings with money using the word 'whom', would be pretty conspicuous. What does Jim Mellor have to say?"

"I can't find Mellor. He's also gone."

"That's too bad. I thought he might have more sense."

"I'll try New York. It isn't possible to look everywhere. Since"

I'm no longer working for the government, I don't have their help."

"You must have enjoyed that conversation we had about spies. I'll bet you got a laugh out of that."

"No. I was impressed by it. You were thoughtful and well-informed, as always."

"What did you think of Sorel's *Reflections on Violence?*"

"Bored the piss out of me."

BJ nodded. "Well, at least it served a useful purpose." Then he frowned. He moved his chair closer to the desk, took off his glasses, and picked up a book. "There's a truth you should face, that I think you need to face."

"What is it?"

"Liz came to me and asked for advice because she was troubled about which path to choose—nonviolent protest, the Gandhi and Martin Luther King approach, or force, explosives. She was undecided. She was more comfortable with nonviolence, but she didn't see it working and she wanted change, she wanted results. I told her that I couldn't really provide an answer, but I suggested that she follow her heart. And then, a short time later, you told her that you were a spy, that you had lied to her—to all of us, but most importantly to her—and that you worked for the CIA and had violated her trust. Can you imagine how that hurt? It wasn't simply the end of a love affair. She'd been betrayed. Her lover had chosen to embrace the imperialist government, the enemy, instead of her. She'd been on the fence, but your revelation pushed her off it. She moved from indecision to rebellion—very understandably, I think. Your disloyalty...I won't call it treachery, but some would call it that. Your disloyalty—I think you have to accept that characterization—made her decision for her. You showed her that the government's side is cruel and unprincipled."

"That's a pretty harsh judgment."

"I think we all need to accept the consequences of our actions. Please close the door as you leave."

Bill put his hand on the doorknob but he had more to say. "BJ, I'm surprised at you. It's more complex than that. "

"What's more complex?"

"The choices I faced. I had conflicting loyalties. I owed a duty to my employer, the CIA. I had promised to serve the nation. Of course, I didn't know when I made that promise that I was going to meet Liz, going to fall in love, but it was an unconditional promise and one that I wanted to carry out. At some point over the months, the conflict became clear to me, but that didn't resolve it, didn't solve the problem. I still had the conflict. I loved Liz, but I had a duty to the CIA. I'd promised to do a job."

"We all have to make choices. Your problem is that you made the wrong one."

"I made the choice. I told Liz the truth. I disobeyed my instructions, my orders from the CIA, and I told Liz the painful truth."

"You should have made that choice sooner."

"You don't think that. You think I shouldn't have gone to work for the CIA in the first place. I suppose if you believe this country is evil, that the nation is unworthy, not worth serving, then the choice is easy. But I don't believe that. I made the choice to tell her only with real anguish. I wish I was as certain about all this as you appear to be. Where is your 'on the one hand, but on the other'?"

BJ put his book down, pushed his chair back from the desk, and put his glasses on so that he could see Bill more clearly. "I think anybody who wants to be a spy has got something wrong with him."

"Yeah, maybe. And I think anybody who wants to be a dope fiend has got something wrong with him."

"That's probably right, too. I hope you find her, for her sake."

February 16, 1970, telephone call to New York City

"Mr. Boudin, this is Willy Feld in Ann Arbor, Michigan. I'm acquainted with your daughter, Kathy. I'm trying to locate a friend of Kathy's, Liz Watson. Liz is my girlfriend, but she's gone away and I'm concerned about her. I can't find her. I thought Kathy might be in touch with Liz. Could you tell me how to contact Kathy?"

"I'm sorry, Mr. Feld, but I don't know where Kathy is these days. My wife and I haven't seen or heard from her since just after the first of the year, and she hasn't returned our calls."

"That sounds like the situation with Liz. She's dropped out of sight. I don't know where she is."

"Maybe they don't want to be found."

"That possibility had occurred to me. If you hear from Kathy or manage to reach her, would you please ask her to contact me?"

"Yes, of course, Mr. Feld."

February 16, 1970, telephone call to New York City

"Bob, this is Bill Burke, your old buddy from Spook School. How are you doing?"

"I'm fine, Bill. What are you up to these days? Still chasing spies?"

"Need to know, Bob. Need to know. Right now I'm trying to find a woman."

"Aren't we all."

"Yeah, but this is serious business. Her name is Liz Watson. She's involved with the Weathermen and they've been moving dynamite around. They bought a hundred pounds of it in New Hampshire and we think they took it to New York. If we can find Liz Watson, we can probably find the dynamite. Rabbit has a file on her. She's originally from a small town in Illinois, but most recently she's been in Ann Arbor. She has Bryn Mawr connections, including Kathy Boudin."

"I know of the Boudins."

"I've been in touch with Leonard Boudin, Kathy's father. He says he doesn't know where she is. As I'm sure you know, the Weathermen have gone underground."

"So I hear."

"That's what this is all about."

"Is the FBI on to this? Looking for Liz Watson?"

"No, I don't think so. Rabbit doesn't want to read them in—part of the feud with Hoover. Nothing I can do about it."

"Bullshit."

"Yeah. I think Liz is probably traveling with a guy named Hal Roberts. Langley has a description and bio. They may well be in your town. If somebody wants to disappear, New York City is a good place to do it. The dynamite, too. If you can find it and them, you can prevent some bombings and be a hero."

"I'll do some digging."

"Thanks, Bob. If you need anything more, let me know. You can still get messages to me through the dark call number. If you get a lead, I'll come to New York and pursue it. But, without a lead, it's the needle in a haystack."

"I'll give it a try."

February 20, 1970, Ann Arbor

Bill walked into the police station and asked at the desk for Carl Rivac. After a few minutes, Rivac emerged from the squad room. He looked at Bill and frowned.

"What are you doing here?"

"I thought you might be willing to help find Liz."

"I saw that the bar is closed."

"Yeah. I think it's probably out of business. Most of the customers stopped coming after the split within SDS. Liz lost her job. Voice went silent."

"Is she still living with you?"

"She was, but we broke up. Long story. Now she's gone and I can't find her."

"Do you want to file a missing person report? She'd have to be gone at least 48 hours."

"We could do that, I suppose, but I thought maybe you could get the FBI involved."

"Why can't you go to the FBI? Are you wanted?"

"No. I don't think so, but you can check that out. I'm not worried about that. This is a national security matter. She's involved with the Weathermen — Hannah Meyer, Bill Bissell, and so on — and they've all gone underground. They've been involved in bombings. I don't think Liz has yet, but there'll be more bombings. I want to get Liz away from them so she won't get hurt. I think you don't want her hurt either."

"No, I don't. You're right about that."

"I think she's probably gone off with a guy named Hal Roberts, a U of M grad student. And maybe Bissell and Meyer. The FBI should be on their trail. They need to be." Rivac was making notes. Then Bill continued. "Liz has parents living in Hiscott, Illinois, but I'm told they haven't heard from her since Christmas."

"I'll do what I can."

Bill wrote a telephone number on a small piece of paper, folded the paper in half, and handed it to Rivac. "Here's a number. If you have any information, call it. I won't be the person who answers, but they'll get a message to me. They may say they don't know me, but just give them the message and it will get to me."

"Who do you work for?"

"That's on a need-to-know basis. But I think you believe me that I just want to help Liz now."

March 1, 1970, a telephone call

"Hey Bill, Bob Metzler here. We got a problem. Langley tells me you're no longer a company man. So they say whatever you're doing, you're doing it on your own."

"Yeah. Well that's mostly true. Except that I think I'm on the payroll for another couple of weeks, but I'm on paid administrative leave or something like that. But that doesn't really change anything."

"Well, it changes that I have to report to Rabbit and follow his instructions."

"The Agency, and the FBI and everybody else, wants to find the Weathermen and the dynamite. Hannah Meyer and most of their leaders are on a wanted list. Hell, even my cover name is on a wanted list."

"Why haven't you been hauled in by the local police?"

"Rabbit blocked it."

"I know why. I'm told that you were the only asset the Agency had inside. Now they've got no one. Neither does the FBI. Nada. That's why they're very pissed off that you went rogue."

"I didn't go rogue, goddamn it. I just want to find Liz. They want to find her, too. We're on the same page, mostly. They sure want the dynamite and Hannah. Liz, Hal Roberts, and the true believers will be nearby. Rabbit will tell you that he wants you to find them."

"He already has. So, yeah, I'll work on it. But it won't be easy. They're dug in. All of my informants have gone quiet. They say they don't know where the biggies are, and maybe they really don't. I persuaded a good-looking girl to set up a breakfast date with Mark Rudd at a coffee house on Orchard, on the Lower East Side. She made the date, but Rudd didn't show. I think he probably got there early and saw something he didn't like, or he was watching the place and smelled something fishy." There was noise on the telephone line. "Anyway, I'll try, but don't count on it."

March 3, 1970, another telephone call

Bill's phone rang.

"Mr. Burke, this is Mary at the company. I've received a message from Carl Rivac in Michigan. He said to tell you that he's been unable to locate the young woman. So far as he can determine, she's not in Ann Arbor or Detroit or nearby."

"Thank you, Mary. I'll continue to be available for messages."

Eight

March 6, 1970, New York City

A townhouse in Greenwich Village exploded. A fire followed and there were then two more explosions in the house. The building was completely destroyed. There was not much left of the two bodies closest to the original explosion, but one was identified from the fingerprints on a severed hand. It was that of a young woman, Liz Watson.

March 8, 1970, telephone call, Bill to Rabbit

On an open line:

"She's dead, Rabbit."

"Yes, I know."

"Do you feel good about that?"

"Don't be insulting. Are you sober?"

"Not entirely, but I see the truth clearly. We could have saved her." Bill drifted away. "We could have saved her."

"How?"

"We should have had the FBI arrest her, pick her up, hold her for cooling off."

"Did you know where she was?"

"No, but I could have told the FBI to find her."

"First of all, the FBI would have found her if they could have. They were looking. And if you'd gone to them, that would have blown your cover, and the FBI would have told us to get the hell out of their business."

"I blew my cover anyway." Bill's voice broke. "This is a pretty terrible world."

"Don't go off the deep end, Bill."

"Don't go off the deep end!" Bill sobbed. "What do you call it when a lovely girl with a good education and high ideals, from a good family, trying to do the right thing, dies because she can't stomach the immorality she sees around her, the immorality of her own country."

"Do you agree with her?"

"Agree with her?" Bill's desk chair squeaked as he tried to find a comfortable position. "Agree with her?" The chair squeaked again as Bill leaned forward, put his elbows on the desk and throttled the phone. "What I know is that she died because of our failings. Her blood is on our hands."

"I should not have taken your call. Sleep it off, Bill. Go on with your life. Don't hurt yourself."

"Take your eyes off that goddamn flag and listen to me! Don't patronize me, you pompous asshole. When you put the telephone down you'll get out your scotch bottle and you'll have three or four drinks and then you'll take the rest of the day off. And to-morrow you'll be back in the office and you'll tell yourself what a fine public servant you are, and when you retire you'll get the Presidential Medal of Freedom and have a lovely dinner at Sans Souci. And Liz is dead."

"Grow up. You knew what our job was. We have a duty to protect the nation. When people decide to kill innocent citizens in order to achieve their goals, and they have the means to do it, we have to stop them. The people that the Weathermen would kill don't deserve to die. The self-appointed killers do deserve it."

"Are you a killer?"

"I will use deadly force, if necessary, within the bounds of the law. Within the bounds of the law!"

"Really? Was the Bay of Pigs within the bounds of the law? What law? How many people died?" Bill coughed. "The explosion in that townhouse did more for you than I could ever have done. Of course if the bomb had exploded at the NCO club dance at Fort Dix, that might have killed off the peace movement totally. Public sympathy would all have been with the soldiers and their families. The Reverend Coffin, Doctor Spock, and Jane Fonda might even have kept their mouths shut. But in some ways this result is even better for you. Three of the Weatherman leaders are dead. It's a miracle that more weren't killed. And the revolution has been thoroughly discredited because the dissidents have been publicly shown, in the most dramatic way, to be willing to kill innocent people, lots of them. The Weather is, in fact, damn scary, and that's now been demonstrated for all to see."

"I didn't kill Liz. She blew herself up. Get that straight." Rabbit hung up.

A week later, Watertown, New York

Bill went home. He was not really from Brooklyn; that was just a cover story. He was from Watertown. And he had graduated from Rochester, not Colgate University as "Willy Feld" had. But Bill's father really was a furniture store owner; that part of the cover story was true. His dad had served in the Army in World War II and he had encouraged Bill's career in the CIA. (There was no practical way to hide Bill's employment from his parents. The Agency instructed parents in the importance of secrecy, and it ran security checks on them.) Bill thought he could talk to his father. He needed someone to talk to. His mother wouldn't understand the violence, and she would be upset by it all, but his father had carried out orders during the war. He would sympathize.

His parents needed to know the basic facts. So the first thing Bill did when he got home was tell them about Liz. The *Watertown Daily Times* had carried a story about the explosion in Greenwich Village, but his parents hadn't been aware that Bill knew any of those people and they certainly had no inkling that his lover had been in the townhouse. Now that Bill's cover had been blown and he was no longer working for the CIA, he could be reasonably open about what he had been doing. Liz had spread the word in Ann Arbor. Bill looked at the floor and seldom met their eyes.

Bill's mother and father could see that he wanted to talk, to open up, but they didn't want to press him. They thought it best to give him time to unwind and come to terms with his obvious sense of loss. They discussed it, several times, and decided that Bill might be more likely to speak freely to his father. That could wait until Bill was ready.

On his mother's bridge club night, Bill and his dad decided that there wasn't enough privacy at the neighborhood bar, so they talked in the family living room. Bill began. He had thought about it. Some of what he said was a rehearsed speech that he had made to himself, in his head, many times.

"When I started the job, I was dedicated to something. It's difficult now to put a name on it, to think what it was. If you asked me why I was doing it, I suppose I might have said I was devoted to 'the country' or 'democracy' or 'justice' or some such, but none of those big things is very close to personal life, very close to me.

"And then there was Liz. Liz was close. If asked whether I wanted love, I would surely have said yes, but I didn't really know what that was in any comprehensive sense. I don't think I know now. Of course I wanted sex, always, but it was more than that. I'm talking about love in a broader, deeper sense, something closer to an appreciation of worth, both my own worth and the other person's, something closer to mutual respect of a lasting and profound kind, the kind that means you care, truly care, about the person. I truly cared about Liz."

Bill's father opened another beer for each of them. Bill continued. "Whatever it was I wanted, I sure didn't get it. Of course I wanted to succeed, not just in the sense of getting ahead, although that would have been fine, but in the sense of doing good work. I wanted my work to be appreciated by Rabbit, but I think—I hope—I wanted something more than that. I wanted the work to have real value. Did that mean lasting value? I don't know. I don't think anyone can see far enough ahead to know what will last. Where will the United States be tomorrow? What will our position be in the world? But I wanted something that made a difference, at least for a time."

Bill drank some beer. "Did I want to help people? Did I want to be of service? Yes, but not in any well-defined way. I may have thought that democracy or justice would help people in general. No doubt I did think that, but I couldn't have specified it more clearly. After a time, I certainly wanted to help Liz. And I failed."

Bill's father asked, "Did you think that what Liz and her friends were doing was right?"

"Are you asking whether Liz and her friends persuaded me, converted me to their cause? Well, I suppose you could say I was persuaded that the United States is doing a lot of bad stuff. Most of that came from the news, not from Liz. Maybe I thought most of that already. But I wasn't persuaded that I could do anything about it. The historical forces that Liz's communist buddies were always talking about produced those evils, and those same forces will continue to produce them."

Bill stared at his beer bottle but didn't drink. "One of my faults was pride, I think. The ambition to produce good work ended up blinding me to what I was sacrificing. The work isn't everything. Other things matter. If you're going to be dedicated to something, it had better not be a false god. That was Liz's problem and it was mine too. My dedication to the Agency and to the country was misplaced. They weren't worthy of it."

His father said, "I'm sorry you feel that way."

Bill's response was a partial answer. "I gave up a lot for my work. Far too much. I gave up Liz's love. I must have known at the time that I was doing that. I'm not so stupid that I wouldn't, couldn't have seen it. But I think I hoped, foolishly, that I could have both. So I have neither. I sure didn't prevent bombs from being built, and there'll probably be more of them. The Weathermen are still out there. Will the country survive? Or democracy? Or justice? Who knows? They're sure not looking good so far. Ask the Vietnamese, ask the Black Panthers, ask John Lewis. Ask Fred Hampton, Martin Luther King, Malcolm X, Jack Kennedy, Bobby Kennedy, Emmet Till, Michael Schwerner, Andrew Goodman, James Chaney. Who else? How many more? What in the hell did I accomplish? I ruined my life, that's for sure. And I didn't save Liz's. She's still gone."

His father said, "I don't agree with all of that, but that doesn't really matter. You're a good man, Bill. You always have been. You'll come through this. I know it. It's a good sign that you thought you could talk to me."

Bill didn't find it all that satisfying.

March 15, 1970, Tupper Lake, NY

The telephone rang.

"Bill Burke please."

"Yes."

"Mr. Burke, this is Harry Watson, Liz's father."

"I'm sorry."

"Our family is too."

"How did you find me?"

"Liz told us that she had a boyfriend named Willy Feld and the Ann Arbor police told us that Feld was really Bill Burke, who worked for the federal government. They said that's now common knowledge in Ann Arbor. A private investigator did the rest. He said it was easy."

"Yes. My former employer is no longer protecting me." Bill pulled out a chair from the kitchen table and sat down.

"Why did she do it, Mr. Burke? My wife and I are stunned, and we can't really talk or think about anything else. You had more contact with her than we did in recent years. We know it's not your fault."

"I loved her. Did she tell you that? I'm still trying to make sense of it. She was a fine person."

"How did she end up in a bomb factory? How could that possibly happen? Was she there under duress? Or was it a suicide, either by Liz or by one of her friends?"

Bill thought that her father deserved to hear the truth. "I've thought about that. The government intelligence report is that the bomb was going to be placed at a non-commissioned officers' club at an army base in New Jersey, at a dance. The bomb was loaded with bolts and nails. Soldiers and their wives would have been killed. It's hard to imagine. She was a lovely, lovely girl—a beautiful person, smart, kind, well-intentioned—but she was making a bomb, or at least she was standing very close to someone who was. The explosion was a shock to the Weathermen. I'm sure of that. My hope is that it took the steam out of them, sobered them."

Harry Watson said, "I wonder whether Liz knew that, whether she had figured that out, so she did it on purpose. She can't have wanted to kill people. Surely now they'll see the cost, the waste." His voice became weak, trailed off. "See that it's all just a fantasy, with nothing good to come of it."

"Mr. Watson, I'd sure like to comfort you. I'm sure you'd like to comfort me. But I don't think the explosion was intentional. It was probably an accident. Somebody attached the wrong wire, closed the circuit." Bill's mouth was dry. He took a sip of coffee. "One of the people she was with, Hal Roberts, was a very bad guy. He died in the explosion. The forensics people say that he was closest to the bomb. He probably attached the wire. I think Hal had a death wish, but not for the way it happened. Do you know that scene at the end of *Butch Cassidy and the Sundance Kid*? The scene where Paul Newman and Robert Redford are being chased by a posse, and the posse, with a whole lot of men, is just outside the building where Butch and Sundance are holed up? So they charge out straight toward the posse and are killed in a hail of gunfire. That scene fascinated Hal. He watched it over and over. I think that's the way he wanted to go—in a head-on charge, killed by a posse in a hail of gunfire. He didn't get his wish. He died, but he didn't get the posse." Bill exhaled, audibly. "I'm pretty sure it was an accident."

Watson sounded exhausted. "I have a photo of Liz in the party dress she wore to the dinner dance we gave in honor of Ellen and Dan a little more than a year ago. Liz looks beautiful, of course. I gave that picture to a newspaper to use with her obituary so that people could see how beautiful she was." He paused. "But the newspaper played the story as 'Debutante Killed in Bomb Factory.'" Watson paused again. Bill remained silent. "She had a good time at the party, I think. She danced with all the eligible men there. You'll understand and forgive me, I hope, if I say that I wish she had taken a fancy to one of them."

"I understand. Maybe, then, she would be alive."

"I'd like to think that she didn't intend to do harm."

"I'm sure she didn't, Mr. Watson, not in the larger sense. I've been thinking about this a lot. I don't want to burden you, but I could give you more of my thoughts."

"Of course, I'd like to hear it."

"Let me begin by saying that I certainly wish Liz had lived many more years. I know you do, too. But I can't help wondering what her life would have been like. You and I would both have tried to make her as happy as possible, but she was set on a disastrous path. I tried to move her off it; I'm sure you did, too. We didn't succeed. Her radical beliefs were genuine and deep. She thought that the United States, her country, was committing acts of aggression that were morally wrong. She even called it 'evil'. The reason she followed Hal wasn't a romantic attachment; she didn't like him. She followed him because he was a strong radical, a comrade. He was devoted to the cause. So was she. If she had lived, and if our bombing in Cambodia continued, what would she have done? She knew that thousands of people are dying in Vietnam and Cambodia. She wanted to stop that. It was a problem of ends and means. I've had to face something like it. I loved her, but I lied to her. I used her as a source of confidential information that I passed on to Langley. She trusted me. I violated that trust. We all make moral choices. Sometimes we make the wrong ones.It's hard to know where to start. Liz is dead. But that's not the start, that's the end. You and your wife have lost your daughter. I've lost the love of my life. How many families in Vietnam have felt the same way? The CIA says I'm unstable. They're right. And Liz is dead."

***

The telephone hung on a wall. For a few minutes, Bill stared at it and at the other things on the wall. His eyes moved slowly. There were a half-dozen framed photos of people he didn't know, probably the family of the couple who owned the place. It was decorated with the usual collection of Adirondack ornament — a mounted deer head (an eight-point buck), two large fish of a kind he didn't recognize, and a flat fungus that grows on trees. The fungus was as big as a plate. Someone had drawn a forest scene on it, not very well.

It was the off-season. A canoe was stored upside down on the dining table. There was no running water. There would be in the summer, but the pipes would freeze at this time of year. He carried water to the house in buckets and big plastic bottles. Strenuous work would be good for him, or so he had been told. Bill had the cabin for a month. A fireplace and two small electric heaters provided what heat there was. The flue didn't draw well, but he'd be damned if he'd clean the chimney. He had wool blankets.

He had tried once again to read *The Big Sleep*. He had read it before, with enjoyment, but it now seemed stale and contrived. The real world was worse than Chandler's confection. Bill walked out onto the screen porch. It was too cold for deep breaths. It was also too cold to sit, and the chairs were still covered for the winter. Most of the windows had plastic over them to keep blowing snow out, but the wind had torn one of the covers, and he could see the lake. There were no boats. Tupper Lake was frozen solid and would be until late April or even early May. In August, when months of sun had warmed the water but the nights were chilly, vapor would condense as it rose into the cold air and the prospect would be veiled in fog, sometimes dense, lasting for an hour or so until the sun was high enough to burn it off. He remembered times when he went out in a canoe before sunrise to watch the mist form and thicken. Now the view of the frozen lake was austere, but beautiful.

Acknowledgments

My constant consultant, Anne Heinz, provided intelligent advice, wise judgments, and needed encouragement every day for two years. Callum Angus did a perceptive substantive edit of the manuscript and offered expert criticism. Ward Just, a friend of long duration and a loyal correspondent, showed how it is done in the big leagues. David Collins read the manuscript with extraordinary care and made dozens of editorial improvements. Linda Hughes edited the final manuscript with a sharp eye, keen perception, and uncommon grace. Anne Godden-Segard was always willing to be helpful with research assistance and manuscript preparation. Friends and family who provided literary advice or thoughtful counsel include Fred Aman, Michael Barsa, William Conger, Peter DiCola, Peter Heinz, David Hilliard, Edward Laumann, Kevin Leonard, Lee Randhava, Rayman Solomon, Mary Sprague, Irvin Slate, and Philip Turner. The Northwestern University libraries provided essential research—Tom Gaylord of the law library was especially helpful. The archives of Northwestern University and the Chicago History Museum supplied valuable material.

Several published sources inform the story. *Diana, the Making of a Terrorist*, by Thomas Powers, is a biography of Diana Oughton — Liz Watson has some of Oughton's characteristics. A few of the prominent Weathermen wrote memoirs, e.g., Bill Ayers, *Fugitive Days: Memoirs of an Antiwar Activist*; Mark Rudd, *Underground: My Life with SDS and the Weathermen*; and Cathy Wilkerson, *Flying Too Close to the Sun: My Life and Times as a Weatherman.* Jerry Rubin's *We Are Everywhere* is a contemporaneous account of the Yippies. There are two plays based on Kathy Boudin, David Mamet's *Anarchist* and Willy Holtzman's *Something You Did*. Kirkpatrick Sale's *SDS* is an authoritative, detailed history of the organization. Michael Arlen's *An American Verdict* is a trenchant account of the killing of Fred Hampton and the resulting trial. William J. Adelman's *Haymarket Revisited* is an account of the Haymarket riot, the prosecutions, and the repeated destruction of the monument. Paul Avrich, *The Haymarket Tragedy*, is a more comprehensive treatment of the same subject. There are also several general treatments of radical politics in the 1960s. Those used in the writing of the novel include Terry H. Anderson, *The Movement and the Sixties: Protest in America from Greensborough to Wounded Knee*; Bryan Burrough, *Days of Rage: America's Radical Underground, the FBI, and the Forgotten Age of Revolutionary Violence;* David Farber, *Chicago '68*; David Farber, *The Age of Great Dreams: America in the 1960s*; Norman Mailer, *Miami and the Siege of Chicago*; and Irwin Unger and Debbi Unger, *Turning Point: 1968*.

Historical Note

Historical fiction is tricky—it is difficult for the reader to know which parts of the story are history and which are fiction. This novel's descriptions of major public events—e.g., the 1967 march on the Pentagon; the 1968 SDS convention in East Lansing; the protests at the 1968 Democratic Party nominating convention; the 1969 SDS meeting at the Chicago Coliseum; the 1969 Days of Rage in Chicago; the National War Council in Flint, Michigan, at the end of 1969; and the 1970 townhouse explosion—are based on the historical record. The action is intended to capture the essence of the real events. There are, however, two departures in the novel from the historical time sequence. The barricading of Sheridan Road at Northwestern University and the arson of the ROTC building at Washington University are loosely based on similar events that took place at those universities, but the actions both occurred in 1970, after the conclusion of the novel.

About the Author

Jack Heinz has published in *Harper's*, *Sports Illustrated*, the *Hudson Review*, and *Adirondack Life*. He has also written essays for catalogues of art exhibits, liner notes for a three-CD album of jazz, and numerous articles in professional journals. His scholarly books have been published by the university presses of Harvard, the University of Chicago, Northwestern, and the University of Illinois. He was the executive director of the American Bar Foundation and is now a research professor emeritus there. He is also the Owen L. Coon professor emeritus at Northwestern University's Pritzker School of Law and an affiliated scholar of Northwestern's Institute for Policy Research. He was an Air Force officer, serving in both the Pentagon and the White House.

He lives in Evanston, Illinois, and in Tupper Lake, New York, on the Stony Creek Ponds. This is his first novel.

CPSIA information can be obtained
at www.ICGtesting.com
Printed in the USA
FSHW011623050519
57863FS